At Issue

# Foster Care

## Other Books in the At Issue Series:

Age of Consent
AIDS in Developing Countries
Are Athletes Good Role Models?
Are Natural Disasters Increasing?
Does Outsourcing Harm America?
Does the Two Party System Still Work?
How Does Religion Influence Politics?
Is Biodiversity Important?
Is Iran a Threat to Global Security?
Nuclear and Toxic Waste
Piracy on the High Seas
Right to Die
Should the Federal Budget Be Balanced?
Should the Federal Government Bail Out Private Industry?
Should the Internet Be Free?
Should the U.S. Close Its Borders?
Should Vaccinations Be Mandatory?
Voter Fraud
What Is the Impact of Emigration?

At Issue

# Foster Care

*Debra Bloom, Book Editor*

**GREENHAVEN PRESS**
*A part of Gale, Cengage Learning*

Detroit • New York • San Francisco • New Haven, Conn • Waterville, Maine • London

Christine Nasso, *Publisher*
Elizabeth Des Chenes, *Managing Editor*



*For more information, contact:*
Greenhaven Press
27500 Drake Rd.
Farmington Hills, MI 48331-3535
Or you can visit our Internet site at gale.cengage.com



Articles in Greenhaven Press anthologies are often edited for length to meet page requirements. In addition, original titles of these works are changed to clearly present the main thesis and to explicitly indicate the author's opinion. Every effort is made to ensure that Greenhaven Press accurately reflects the original intent of the authors. Every effort has been made to trace the owners of copyrighted material.



**LIBRARY OF CONGRESS CATALOGING-IN-PUBLICATION DATA**

Foster care / Debra Bloom, editor.
p. cm. -- (At issue)
Includes bibliographical references and index.
978-0-7377-4514-6 (hardcover)
978-0-7377-4515-3 (pbk.)
1. Children--Institutional care. 2. Foster home care. I. Bloom, Debra.
HV713.F67 2009
362.73'3--dc22

2009023048

Printed in the United States of America
1 2 3 4 5 6 7 13 12 11 10 09

# Contents

# Introduction

In April 2008, 440 children were removed from the Yearning for Zion (YFZ) ranch in Eldorado, Texas. After receiving calls from the YFZ compound, which alleged sexual and physical abuse of children, Texas Child Protective Services took custody of the children from the YFZ facility, owned by the Fundamentalist Church of Jesus Christ of Latter-Day Saints. The children and their parents became participants in the largest child custody hearing in Texas history. As the *Houston Chronicle* reported on April 28, 2008, "An army of lawyers and case workers are working to sort out the legal and social services issues in the case of the removal of hundreds of children from the Eldorado polygamist sect ranch." The case acutely highlights the complicated system of agencies and officials that have evolved into the modern child welfare system.

Today's foster care system was not always an intricate array of government organizations and child welfare advocates. An awareness of the need for child welfare began after the American Civil War. According to Civilwarhome.com, over six hundred thousand soldiers died between 1861 and 1865; include civilian deaths and the Civil War accounted for more deaths than all other U.S. wars combined, from the Revolution through Vietnam. One result of the war casualties was a significant population of orphans. Without a government agency to help assist broken families it became the mission of caring Americans to help these children.

Philanthropist Charles Loring Brace was concerned with the welfare of poor children. He and other reformers formed the Children's Aid Society (CAS) to help orphans living on the streets of New York City. Financial support for the CAS came from private donations. The CAS, along with other charity organizations, worked to help needy families by providing inexpensive housing, schools, summer camps, and sanitariums in New York City.

The CAS was not without its critics. Much like today's foster care system, it was accused of singling out a particular group—in this case, Catholics. Catholic children were removed from their "inadequate" surroundings and taken to Protestant homes via a program called the Orphan Trains. Between 1854 and 1929, the Orphan Trains moved nearly two hundred and fifty thousand children to families in the Midwest. The *Adoption History Project* biography of Brace explains that, "Not surprisingly, an ideology that seemed benevolent and humanitarian to many Protestants earned Brace a reputation in Catholic communities as a child-stealer rather than a child-saver."

Despite criticism, these early humanitarian groups alerted civic leaders to the plight of America's children. Concerned citizens, including social workers and reform advocates Lillian Wald and Florence Kelley, met to discuss what role the federal government should play in keeping abandoned children off the streets and put into safe homes. Their meetings culminated in 1912 with the passage of legislation creating the Children's Bureau, America's first government agency organized for the protection of children.

The federal role in child welfare services began in earnest with the Social Security Act of 1935 which created the Aid to Dependent Children (ADC). The ADC became part of the Social Security Administration in 1946 as health issues for children became more prominent. In 1962, the foster care component was added to ADC with federal money to distribute to states for foster care payments.

Several major federal legislative acts have been created according to the Pew Commission on Children in Foster Care, which developed recommendations for the foster care system from 2003 to 2006. One such piece of legislation is the Indian

Child Welfare Act, which was enacted to reduce the high number of Native American children in the foster care system. Tribes and tribal courts were given greater jurisdiction in overseeing the welfare of native children and federal money was provided to help protect and stabilize Native American homes.

The Adoption Assistance and Child Welfare Act of 1980 was a major legislative act that required states to become more involved in the child welfare system. The act required states to develop standardized procedures for placing children in foster care and to develop strategies for keeping families together.

The Adoption and Safe Families Act (ASFA) was the first of two major pieces of foster care legislation enacted during the President Bill Clinton administration. The legislation addressed three child welfare issues:

- Children continued to remain in foster care too long;
- The child welfare system was biased toward family preservation at the expense of children's safety and well-being; and
- Inadequate attention and resources were devoted to adoption as a permanent placement option for abused and neglected children.

While signing the legislation into law on November 19, 1997, President Clinton said, "The new legislation makes it clear that children's health and safety are the paramount concerns of our public child welfare system. It makes it clear that good foster care provides important safe havens for our children, but it is by definition a temporary, not a permanent, setting."

While legislation at the turn of the twentieth century focused on the physical needs of children, the concern, over time, has shifted to the importance of child protection. Examples of modern foster care issues include: lack of foster parents, teens aging out of the foster care system, parental substance abuse, and racial inequalities in foster care placements.

As new concerns arise, legislation is enacted to produce helpful programs. Despite the constant stream of new legislation, however, there is concern that the foster care system is ineffective and needs reform. Nina Bernstein, in the introduction to *The Lost Children of Wilder: The Epic Struggle to Change Foster Care*, asserts, "The two hundred year history of American child welfare is littered with programs once hailed as reforms and later decried as harmful or ineffective, only to emerge again in the guise of new solutions to past problems." In *At Issue: Foster Care*, the authors provide insight into the current foster care system and solutions for problems, old and new.

1

# Foster Care: An Overview

***Tom Harris***

*Tom Harris is a staff writer for the HowStuffWorks Web site.*

*Just as there are diverse family structures, there are a myriad of reasons that some children cannot remain with their biological families, and foster care is one temporary solution. Although the federal government enacts legislation that provides funding and guidelines for foster care, individual programs are organized at the state and county levels. Caseworkers supervise foster parents and children during the initial placements and then continue to work for reunification with family members or adoption. There are varieties of care for foster children based on their particular needs: they may require short- or long-term care, legal assistance, emotional or psychological assistance, emergency housing, or special group housing.*

We generally think of childhood in terms of the nuclear family. Mom and dad, or just mom or just dad, take care of their kids. But the reality is things don't always work out this way. For any number of reasons, parents sometimes end up in a situation where they can't take care of their children, either temporarily or permanently. What happens then?

Throughout history, the fate of these children has depended wholly on the goodwill of the community. In the past, if extended family, neighbors or strangers didn't step in as surrogate parents, parentless children would be turned out on the streets. Today, this sort of community childcare is institu-

Tom Harris, "How Foster Care Works," HowStuffWorks.com, June 29, 2004. Reproduced by permission. http://people.howstuffworks.com.

tionalized, but it still relies on the kindness and compassion of individual members of the community.

In this article, we'll examine one of the cornerstones of modern institutionalized childcare—the foster care system. We'll find out how children enter foster care, how adults sign on as foster parents and how social services regulates the process. If you've ever wondered how you can help kids in need of a home, this article will get you started by introducing you to the foster care system.

## Foster Fundamentals

When parents are unable, unwilling or unfit to care for a child, the child must find a new home. In some cases, there is little or no chance a child can return to their parents' custody, so they need a new permanent home. In other situations, children only need a temporary home until their parents' situation changes. In any case, the children need somewhere to stay until a permanent home is possible. Hundreds of years ago, providing this temporary home fell informally to families, neighbors and often to the church. As cities grew larger and more and more children in a community ended up in this unfortunate situation, government institutions took up much of the responsibility.

Up until relatively recently, the prevailing official approach was to put children in orphanages and poorhouses. If the child was lucky, a loving family would eventually adopt them from the orphanage. Alternatively, a less suited family would take the child on, often to use them for free labor, or the child would stay in the orphanage until reaching adulthood.

Over the past hundred years, the trend in North America and Europe has shifted away from orphanages and towards foster homes. The underlying philosophy of foster care is that children are better off, emotionally and psychologically, in a home environment, with someone filling the role of a parent. The logic is that with one or more foster parents taking care of a smaller number of children, the child should have more of the attention and love they need to grow into healthy adults. Today, there are roughly half a million U.S. children in the foster care system.

---

*Foster care involves a lot of hard work on the part of administrators, social workers, parents and, most importantly, foster children.*

---

## Foster Care or Adoption

Foster care and adoption both provide family environments for children who can't be with their biological parents, but it's important to understand that they are very different institutions. While foster parents are encouraged to connect emotionally with the children in their care, foster families are not meant to be permanent replacements for biological families. In most cases, the ultimate goal is to reunite children with their biological families, as soon as the family is able and fit. This could be as short as a few days or as long as a few years.

Failing family reunification, the ultimate goal is to find adoptive parents who will take on all the emotional and legal responsibilities of birth parents. In the eyes of the law, adopting a child is pretty much the same thing as giving birth to them. Fostering a child, on the other hand, doesn't give the foster parents any major authority over the child's life.

On occasion, foster parents will eventually adopt foster children in their care, but more often, the foster home is a means of returning the child to his or her birth parents or a stop on the way to another home. Unfortunately, many children end up bouncing from foster home to foster home, never finding a permanent family. In this regard, the foster care system is clearly imperfect, since it often adds more instability to a child's life.

The fundamental mission of the foster care system, then, is very simple. Actually putting it into action is another matter. Foster care involves a lot of hard work on the part of administrators, social workers, parents and, most importantly, foster children. In the next couple sections, we'll find out a little about life in this world.

## The Organization

In the United States, foster care operates on the local level, rather than on the national level. The structure varies somewhat from state to state, as do the specific names for government agencies and programs, but most states follow the same general model.

In most cases, the state's division of social services, part of the state department of health and human services, heads up the entire system. These agents oversee county social services departments as well as private foster care agencies. This is one of the most misunderstood facts of foster care: While government regulations generally direct how foster care operates, independent nonprofit organizations (licensed by the state) do a huge amount of the actual work in some areas. These organizations generally receive government funds, but they may also depend on charitable donations.

It's up to the county departments and the private agencies to take care of the details of foster care. Adhering to the state's specific regulations, caseworkers with local organizations train foster parents, place children in foster homes, work with families towards reunification, work with local adoption agencies to find new permanent homes for children and generally keep track of everything involved in each foster child's progress through the system.

Foster care agencies typically consider the group of people working with a particular child as a team. The core members of the team are the foster parents, the biological parents, the court, the social worker in charge of the case and, most importantly, the child him or herself. The team's job is to look out for the best interests of the child and work towards putting the child in a permanent home.

In addition to this core group, several other volunteers and professionals may become part of the team from time to time. For example, an attorney with the state Office of the Child Advocate may represent the child legally, and the court may also assign a Court Appointed Special Advocate, a volunteer who studies the case and supports the child in court.

## Types of Foster Care

There are a number of different types of foster care. In *traditional care*, a relatively small number of children stay with a family or a single foster parent in their home for a matter of months or years. Traditional foster care may also operate on a short-term basis, of a few days to a month, for children who will be reunited with their families quickly.

*Emergency foster homes* are available 24 hours a day to take children in until the social services system can figure out a longer term solution. If a child's parents were arrested, for example, social services might put the child in an emergency foster home until they could locate relatives or find another place for the child.

*Respite foster care families* take children in for a couple days at a time, to give stressed families a periodic break. *Relief care families* work similarly, taking foster children for a short period of time to give their regular foster families a break.

Some foster children live in a *group home* instead of a traditional foster home. Foster care group homes function less like conventional families, and more like dormitories. While foster care agencies prefer to place children with families, a shortage of foster parents means many children end up in this sort of home. Additionally, foster care agencies may place children with special needs in group homes where they can get the professional assistance they need.

The predominant form of foster care is still ordinary people serving as foster parents. In the next section, we'll look at the typical process of becoming a foster parent.

*Serving as a foster parent generally means working closely with a foster agency on a regular basis, and often means regular contact with a child's biological family as well.*

## Becoming a Foster Parent

If you're new to the world of foster care, the prospect of becoming a foster parent can be pretty intimidating. Foster parents are often called "parents plus" because in addition to providing the food, shelter, care, and love a good parent would provide for their own kids, they also have to deal with the special circumstances of a foster child.

Serving as a foster parent generally means working closely with a foster agency on a regular basis, and often means regular contact with a child's biological family as well. Foster children may also have special psychological needs. Many come from abusive environments, and all are in the stressful situation of being apart from their birth family. Additionally, foster parents generally take care of the children for a short time, which can be very difficult emotionally.

But as challenging as this role is, it can also be highly rewarding. Good foster parents know they've provided a home for a child in dire need, and the best ones may even turn a child's entire life around. And nobody in the U.S. foster care system goes in completely unprepared. To take in foster children through a foster agency, you have to go through a screening, training and licensing process.

Foster parents don't have to be married, and prior child-rearing experience is not a necessity. But in most states, they do have to meet the following criteria:

- They must be 21 years or older. Additionally, some states do not accept foster parents who are older than 65.
- They must have room for a child in their home. Some programs require every foster child have his or her own room, while some only require that they have their own bed and personal storage space.
- They must already have the financial resources to provide for their own family.
- They must provide a home that meets certain safety standards.
- They must be in good physical and mental health. . . .

The foster parent does not carry all responsibility for the child, as a biological or adopted parent would. The foster parent is not legally responsible for the child, and may request that the child be removed from the foster home at any time. Medicaid covers the child's medical expenses, and the foster care agency provides a monthly check to help cover the child's room and board. The monthly sum is not by any means extravagant, so foster families may end up supporting the child with their own funds as well. As a point of reference, the recommended monthly rates in North Carolina are:

- $315 for children up to 5 years old
- $365 for children 6 to 12
- $415 for children 13 and up

Even though the state maintains true custody, foster parents do have a definite responsibility for children in their care. Their ultimate responsibilities are to care for the child and to look after his or her daily well-being. In a very real sense, their job is to provide parental love to children without parents.

2

# Children Are in Foster Care Because They Are Poor

***Gaylynn Burroughs***

*Gaylynn Burroughs is a staff attorney in the family defense practice at the Bronx Defenders in New York City.*

*While social workers cite neglect as the most common reason for removing children from their families, they do not make a distinction between abusive family situations and those that are simply too poor to endure. The system focuses on poor families in particular because they have fewer resources to protect their families and they are more visible as recipients of public aid and services. To reduce the number of children in foster care, government policy should focus more attention and resources on the issues of poverty that disrupt otherwise unified families.*

When a recurrent plumbing problem in an upstairs unit caused raw sewage to seep into her New York City apartment, 22-year-old Lisa (not her real name) called social services for help. She had repeatedly asked her landlord to fix the problem, but he had been unresponsive. Now the smell was unbearable, and Lisa feared for the health and safety of her two young children.

When the caseworker arrived, she observed that the apartment had no lights and that food was spoiling in the refrigerator. Lisa explained that she did not have the money to pay her electric bill that month, but would have the money in a

Gaylynn Burroughs, "Too Poor to Parent," *Ms. Magazine*, vol. 18, Spring 2008, pp. 43–45. 

few weeks. She asked whether the caseworker could help get them into a family shelter. The caseworker promised she would help—but left Lisa in the apartment and took the children, who were then placed in foster care.

Months later, the apartment is cleaned up. Lisa still does not have her children.

Monique (also a pseudonym), too, lost her children to foster care despite all her efforts to keep her family united. The impoverished Georgia mother of three had been left by her boyfriend after discovering that their infant son needed heart surgery. Undeterred, she sent her older children to live with family out of state, while she moved to a shelter close to the hospital. When the baby recovered, she moved to New York and was reunited with her other kids.

Unemployed and without financial resources, Monique hoped to live with family, but when they couldn't take her in she looked for a shelter again. This time, though, she got caught up in endless red tape from the emergency housing *and* medical systems—the latter of which kept her waiting months for an appointment with a cardiologist and medication for her child.

---

*Poor families are up to 22 times more likely to be involved in the child-welfare system than wealthier families.*

---

Finally, settled in an apartment loaned by a friend, Monique began a job search, leaving the baby at home with a sitter—and that's when the *real* nightmare began. One day police found the baby alone and took him into protective custody. The next day, child-welfare officials charged Monique with inadequate guardianship *and* medical neglect (because the child hadn't seen a cardiologist or gotten his medication), and put all three children in foster care. Monique can now visit them only once a week, supervised, for just two hours.

## Parenting and Poverty

It is probably fair to say that most women with children worry about their ability as mothers. Are they spending enough time with them? Are they disciplining them correctly? Are they feeding them properly? When should they take them to the doctor, and when is something not that serious? But one thing most women in the United States do not worry about is the possibility of the state removing children from their care. For a sizable subset of women, though—especially poor black mothers like Lisa and Monique—that possibility is very real.

Black children are the most overrepresented demographic in foster care nationwide. According to the U.S. Government Accountability Office (GAO), blacks make up 34 percent of the foster-care population, but only 15 percent of the general child population. In 2004, black children were more than twice as likely to enter foster care as white children. Even among other minority groups, black mothers are more likely to lose their children to the state than Hispanics or Asians—groups that are slightly underrepresented in foster care.

The reason for this disparity? Study after study reviewed by Northwestern University law professor Dorothy Roberts in her book *Shattered Bonds: The Color of Child Welfare* shows that poverty is the leading cause of children landing in foster care. According to one researcher, poor families are up to 22 times more likely to be involved in the child-welfare system than wealthier families. And nationwide, blacks are four times more likely than other groups to live in poverty.

---

*These [poor] mothers are told that they neglected their children by failing to provide adequate food, clothing, shelter, education or medical care.*

---

But when state child-welfare workers come to remove children from black mothers' homes, they rarely cite poverty as the factor putting a child at risk. Instead, these mothers are told that they neglected their children by failing to provide adequate food, clothing, shelter, education or medical care. The failure is always personal, and these mothers and children are almost always made to suffer individually for the consequences of one of the United States' most pressing social problems.

## Antipoverty Services Need Funding

Federal spending for foster care skyrocketed in the 1980s, but funding for antipoverty services to prevent foster-care placement—or speed reunification with birth parents—stagnated. As explained by child-welfare expert Martin Guggenheim, a professor at New York University School of Law, "Between 1981 and 1983, federal foster-care spending grew by more than 400 percent in real terms, while preventive and reunification spending grew by only 14 percent, and all other funds available for social services to the poor declined."

As a result of the failure to fund programs servicing poor families—helping them secure housing, jobs, health care, subsidized day care, mental health services and drug treatment programs—the number of poor children in foster care began to soar. In 1986, the foster care population numbered around 280,000 children. Just five years later, that number had jumped by 53 percent to 429,000. The latest data available shows an estimated 514,000 children in foster care.

Troubled not only by the number of children in foster care but by their longer stays in the system, Congress passed the Adoption and Safe Families Act (ASFA) in 1997. Its purpose is to achieve a permanent family environment more quickly for children in foster care, but the legislation accomplishes that goal by placing time limits on family reunification—thus encouraging adoption instead of the return of children to their parents.

Supporters of ASFA claim that the legislation is child-friendly because it measures time from the perspective of a child's development, and strives to place children in safe homes away from "bad parents" who are unlikely to stop putting their children in harm's way. Certainly there are situations in which temporarily placing a child in foster care, or even terminating parental rights, is the only responsible outcome. However, as Guggenheim points out, "ASFA makes no distinction between parents whose children were removed because of parental abuse and parents whose only crime is being too poor to raise their children in a clean and safe environment without additional benefits the government refuses to supply."

While ASFA was making it more difficult for some parents to win back their children, changes in federal antipoverty policies were making it more difficult for families struggling to keep their children. President [Bill] Clinton's welfare reform in the mid-1990s eliminated federal cash assistance for single mothers and their children in favor of block grants to states, so individual states now have wide discretion to set benefit levels, establish work requirements for welfare assistance and create time limits for public assistance. For some women, the effect of welfare reform was a low-paying job or unemployment, coupled with the loss of a government safety net. Still poor, many of these women continued to lose their children because of the predictable consequences of poverty: lack of health care, inadequate housing and simply the inability to meet basic needs.

## Negative Stereotypes Are No Help

Yet public perception of parents accused of neglecting their children remains extremely negative, regardless of the actual allegations. Child-welfare workers in New York City, citing emergency conditions, routinely remove poor children from their homes without notifying the parents, without securing a court order and without informing parents of their legal rights. Sometimes they even remove children from school, day care or a friend's home without giving parental notice. It's not uncommon in court on Monday morning to meet frantic parents whose children were removed on Friday night and have still not learned where their children were taken. Someone must not think that these parents love their children and actually care to know.

The legal system often provides no haven for these parents. Based on even the flimsiest allegations, they are essentially presumed guilty and pressured to participate in various cookie-cutter services that often do not directly address the concerns that brought them to court. For example, after her children went into foster care, Lisa was asked to attend parenting classes, undergo a mental health evaluation, seek therapy and submit to random drug testing before her children could be returned. But child-welfare authorities did not assist her in repairing her home or finding a new apartment, nor have they gone after her landlord for allowing deplorable conditions. Lisa's poverty has led government authorities to pathologize her; she's automatically considered sick, careless or otherwise unfit if she attempts to parent while poor.

---

*Poor mothers must cope . . . with the crushing gaze of the state, which is too willing to blame its own shortcomings in addressing child poverty on poor women.*

---

And what about children who are physically or sexually abused by their parents? A myth of child welfare is that foster care is full of such children, but in fact the majority of children who encounter the child welfare system have *not* been abused. At least 60 percent of child welfare cases in this country involve solely allegations of neglect.

Lacking private resources, poor women may also come to the attention of government authorities more often than other mothers do, as they must often rely on public services such as shelters, public hospitals and state welfare offices. That gives government workers more opportunities to judge, and report on, parental fitness. So poor mothers must cope not only with the daily frustrations of parenting but with the crushing gaze of the state, which is too willing to blame its own shortcomings in addressing child poverty on poor women and their "bad mothering."

A 2007 report by the GAO on the overrepresentation of black children in foster care, prepared at the request of Rep. Charles B. Rangel (D-N.Y.), showed that most states were making efforts to address racial bias within their child-welfare systems by recruiting more culturally sensitive staff and providing better training to caseworkers. However, bias may be only one factor affecting racial disproportionality, and just a smattering of states have implemented programs to address other factors—such as partnering with community organizations to offer targeted services to black families at risk of losing children to foster care.

Race and poverty should not be a barrier to raising one's children. But in order to prevent the entry of poor children into the foster care system, state and federal government must confront poverty-related issues. In 2006, the federal government spent about $6.8 billion in Title IV-E grants for foster-care-related programs—but only $700 million in Title IV-B grants, which cover adoption, child-protection *and* family-preservation services. States may also use federal block grants to provide preventive services to poor families, but the allocation of these funds is entirely discretionary—and one study found that in 2004 eight states spent none of their block grant from Temporary Assistance for Needy Families on child welfare.

Until this disparity in funding and services is addressed, and until this country comes to terms with its culpability in allowing widespread poverty to exist, poor black mothers will continue to lose their children to the state. And we will continue to label these women "bad mothers" to assuage our own guilt.

# 3

# Children Are in Foster Care Because of Parents' Substance Abuse

***Joseph P. Ryan, Jeanne C. Marsh, Mark F. Testa, and Richard Louderman***

*Joseph P. Ryan is an assistant professor, Mark F. Testa is an associate professor, and Richard Louderman is a research associate in the School of Social Work at the University of Illinois at Urbana-Champaign. Jeanne C. Marsh is dean of the School of Social Services Administration at the University of Chicago.*

*Alcohol and drug abuse is a major problem for families in the foster care system. Children with substance abusing parents stay in foster care longer and have less of a chance of returning to their families. Barriers to proper substance abuse treatment include problems with child care, transportation, and program completion; and child welfare agencies are addressing these problems by incorporating substance abuse programs with other child welfare services. One solution involves recovery coaches who provide individualized support and supervision, often with the ultimate goal of reunification for the recovering individual's family.*

The effective collaboration of multiple service systems to deal with parental alcohol and other drug abuse (AODA) continues to challenge government efforts to ensure family permanence and the safety and well-being of neglected and

Joseph P. Ryan, Jeanne C. Marsh, Mark F. Testa, and Richard Louderman, "Integrating Substance Abuse Treatment and Child Welfare Services: Findings from the Illinois Alcohol and Other Drug Abuse Waiver Demonstration," *Social Work Research*, vol. 30, June 2006, pp. 95–97, 103–106. 

abused children. Research has documented the heavy toll that parental drug addiction exacts on families and children who come to the attention of state child protection authorities. . . . At least 50% of the nearly 1 million children indicated for child abuse and neglect in 1995 had caregivers who abused alcohol or other drugs. A 1994 report issued by the U.S. General Accounting Office (GAO) estimated that the percentage of foster home placements resulting in part from parental drug use rose from 52% to 78% between 1986 and 1991 in the cities of Los Angeles, New York, and Philadelphia. A 1998 GAO study of child protection systems in Los Angeles and Cook County, Illinois, documented that substance use was a problem in more than 70% of active foster care cases. If child welfare systems are to achieve desirable permanency and safety outcomes, the development of innovative service strategies and agency partnerships are necessary.

Parental substance abuse often compromises appropriate parenting practices, creates problems in the parent-child relationship, and significantly increases the risk of child maltreatment. Once involved in the child welfare system, substance-abusing parents are more likely to experience subsequent allegations of maltreatment compared with non-substance-abusing parents. In addition to the increased risk of maltreatment, access to and engagement with treatment providers is often limited. Consequently, children of substance-abusing parents remain in substitute care for significantly longer periods of time and experience significantly lower rates of family reunification relative to almost every other subgroup of families in the child welfare system.

## Access to Treatment Program Is Limited

Access to substance abuse treatment is limited for substance-abusing parents. Overall, in the United States approximately one-third of all individuals who need treatment receive it. The supply of treatment services for women with children is especially inadequate. Problems with child care are known to limit women's access to treatment. Women with children often do not participate in outpatient substance abuse treatment because they are unable to obtain child care. In addition, parents, more than nonparents, remain in residential treatment for shorter periods of time. Lack of adequate transportation is also known to be a significant barrier to treatment access for both women and men. Once enrolled in treatment, many clients—especially parents involved in the child welfare system—fail to complete it. For these reasons, substance-abusing parents in the child welfare system require significant outreach and support throughout the treatment process. . . .

## Recovery Coach Study

The Illinois AODA Waiver Demonstration Project tested a model of intensive case management using recovery coaches. The use of recovery coaches is intended to increase access to substance abuse services, improve substance abuse treatment outcomes, shorten length of time in substitute care placement, and affect child welfare outcomes, including increasing rates of family reunification.

To achieve these stated goals, recovery coaches engage in a variety of activities, including comprehensive clinical assessments, advocacy, service planning, outreach, and case management. The clinical assessments focus on a variety of problem areas, such as housing, domestic violence, parenting, mental health, and family support needs. *Advocacy* refers to assisting parents in obtaining benefits and in meeting the responsibilities and mandates associated with the benefits. Outreach activities ensure that recovery coaches work with substance-abusing families in their communities. Recovery coaches visit the family home and the AODA treatment provider agencies. Recovery coaches also make joint home visits with child welfare caseworkers, AODA agency staff, or both. At least one recovery coach is always on call during evenings, weekends, and holidays to address emergencies. Recovery coaches also have access to outreach or tracker staff that specialize in identifying and engaging hard-to-reach or -locate parents. Finally, recovery coaches share information with child welfare and juvenile court personnel. The information sharing is intended to inform permanency decisions. Recovery coach services are provided for the duration of the case, and such services may also be continued for a period of time subsequent to the case's closing.

Empirical evidence supports the development and implementation of a recovery coach model in child welfare. Evidence shows that clients achieve better outcomes (for example, stay in treatment longer, complete treatment at higher rates) when assigned to individual counselors. This is especially true when such counselors are experts in a particular area of need. Rather than refer and connect families with outside experts, an individual counselor, such as a recovery coach, offers a specialized orientation that is essential for working effectively with families. . . .

## Family Reunification

We focused on two outcomes: access to substance abuse treatment and family reunification. The results indicate that families receiving recovery coach services were more likely to gain access to substance abuse treatment. The results also indicate that families receiving recovery coach services were more likely to achieve family reunification. Specifically, the odds of achieving reunification were 1.28 times greater for families assigned to the recovery coach group.

These are important findings and make a unique contribution to the literature because very few substance-abusing families in the child welfare system achieve family reunification; there are almost no experimental studies of effective interventions for substance-abusing families in the child welfare system; and recent legislation makes it clear that if family reunification is still the primary goal for child welfare systems, the timeline and milestones associated with recovery from substance abuse must coincide with the timeline associated with permanence and the termination of parental rights.

*The culture in family courts, risk-averse judges, and co-existing problems within the family system may all contribute to low reunification rates for children in substance-abusing homes.*

The likelihood of achieving family reunification for substance-abusing parents is extremely low. Of all children entering foster care in 1994, only 19% were still in care as of June 30, 2000 (approximately six years). In comparison, 86% of substance-exposed infants entering care in 1994 failed to return home before January 2002 (approximately 7.5 years). Interventions that can increase the likelihood of family reunification should be considered by state child welfare agencies, even if such increases are modest. In the present study, 12% of the families receiving recovery coach services achieved family reunification (relative to 7% in the control group). This 12% certainly does not reflect the ideal, but considered within the historical context of family reunification for substance-abusing families in Illinois, this percentage is not entirely discouraging. No single intervention will resolve all the issues associated with reunification for substance-abusing families. Furthermore, this study represents interim findings. The AODA waiver demonstration will continue for another two years. If the use of recovery coach services can continue to produce small gains, the accrued differences may be both statistically and clinically significant.

It is also important to note that many factors contribute to reunification. One should not assume that treatment gains are the sole determinant of reunification. Similarly, one should not assume that low rates of reunification are the result of ineffective services. The culture in family courts, risk-averse judges, and coexisting problems within the family system may all contribute to low reunification rates for children in substance-abusing homes. . . .

## Negative Impacts of the Correctional System

The focus of this study was on the effectiveness of the recovery coach model in child welfare. Yet, an additional finding emerged. Family reunification is less likely to occur when parents are simultaneously involved with the adult correctional system. This is an important finding because although the problem of parental arrest or incarceration is well documented in the child welfare literature, there is scant research with regard to the outcomes associated with this particular problem. Recent estimates indicate that approximately 16% of mothers with children in foster care are arrested within 18 months of placement. These arrests are more likely to occur after children are removed from the home. The current study makes a contribution to the literature by moving beyond the descriptive nature of parental involvement with adult corrections and estimating the relationship of such involvement with family reunification.

The finding that simultaneous legal problems decrease the probability of reunification is important for at least two reasons. First, family reunification is a primary objective for children in substitute care placement. The vast majority of children entering the foster care system have an initial permanency goal of "return home." Thus, it is important for policy makers and practitioners to understand the factors that may prevent families from achieving this objective. Moreover, this finding is further evidence that child welfare scholars must look beyond the child welfare system when developing models to explain key child welfare outcomes.

## Integrated Treatment Is Needed

Achieving family reunification for substance-abusing parents in the child welfare system requires innovative and integrated treatment strategies. The Illinois demonstration waiver is a model of service integration that focuses on intensive case management to link child welfare clients to substance abuse services. Our evaluation of this demonstration indicates that substance abuse services can be obtained more quickly and the likelihood of reunification can be slightly increased. The continued development and evaluation of new models of service delivery are necessary if states are to fulfill their obligation to move these families fairly and humanely to permanent situations.

# 4

# Staying in a Troubled Home Can Be Better than Foster Care Placement

***Joseph J. Doyle Jr.***

*Joseph J. Doyle Jr. studies social policy as an economics professor at Massachusetts Institute of Technology's Sloan School of Management.*

*Little is known about the direct effects of foster care on children, but those with experience in foster environments are more prone to delinquency and subsequent homelessness. Observations of children in the child welfare system—with special attention paid to delinquency, teen pregnancy, and employment status and wages—suggest that those on the margin of foster care placement tend to have better outcomes when they remain at home, and this is especially true for older children.*

The child welfare system aims to protect children thought to be abused or neglected by their parents. Over two million children are investigated for child abuse and neglect each year in the United States, and roughly half are found to have been abused. Approximately 10 percent of these abused children will be placed in protective custody known as foster care.

Although foster care is meant to be a temporary arrangement, children stay in care for an average of two years, and there are currently over 500,000 children in care. Roughly 60

Joseph J. Doyle Jr., "Child Protection and Child Outcomes: Measuring the Effects of Foster Care," *The American Economic Review*, vol. 97, December 2007, pp. 1583–1608. 

percent of foster children return home; 15 percent are adopted; and the remainder "age out" of foster care. Three-quarters of these children live with substitute families, one-third of which are headed by relatives of the children. These families are paid a subsidy of approximately $400 per month per child, and states spend over $20 billion each year to administer these child protective services.

Further, foster care policy directly targets children who appear to be at high risk of poor life outcomes. Abused children are three times more likely to die in childhood, with 1,400 child deaths each year directly attributed to child abuse. Those placed in foster care are far more likely than other children to commit crimes, drop out of school, join welfare, experience substance abuse problems, or enter the homeless population. In particular, nearly 20 percent of young prison inmates and 28 percent of homeless individuals spent some time in foster care as a youth . . .

---

*Although an abusive family environment is undoubtedly harmful to child development, removing a child from home may be traumatic as well.*

---

## Foster Care and Child Development

Despite the large number of children at high risk of poor life outcomes served by child protective services, it is unclear whether removing children from home and placing them in foster care is beneficial or harmful for child development, especially for children at the margin of placement. Child protection agencies trade off two competing goods: family preservation and child protection. Although an abusive family environment is undoubtedly harmful to child development, removing a child from home may be traumatic as well. For example, placement instability in foster care has been highlighted as a potentially serious problem for child development.

The average foster child is moved from one home to another at least once, with a quarter experiencing three or more moves.

There are two main limitations to estimating the effects of foster care placements on child outcomes. First, there is a lack of long-term outcome data. Children investigated for abuse or neglect are not tracked over time in a systematic way. Second . . . worse outcomes for foster children compared to other children in the same area could be due to abusive family backgrounds, as opposed to any effect of foster care placement. Meanwhile, those children who are removed are likely those who would benefit most from placement, and a comparison of average outcomes may overstate the benefit of removal for marginal cases.

This [viewpoint] uses a measure of the removal tendency of child protection investigators as an instrumental variable to identify causal effects of foster care placement on child outcomes for school-age children and youth. Cases are distributed to investigators on a rotational basis within geographic field teams to smooth the caseload, which effectively randomizes families to investigators. The instrumental variables estimates focus on variation in foster care placement among marginal cases—those cases where investigators may disagree about the recommendation of removal. These are the cases most likely to be affected by policy changes that alter the threshold for placement.

Using a unique dataset that links children in Illinois with a wide range of government programs, it is possible to compare children placed in foster care with other children who were investigated for abuse or neglect in terms of long-term outcomes, including juvenile delinquency, teen motherhood, employment, and earnings. The results, which apply in particular to children receiving welfare benefits and between the ages of 5 and 15 at the time of the initial investigation, point to better outcomes when children on the margin of placement remain at home. While the large size of the estimated effects and their lack of precision suggest caution in the interpretation, the results suggest that significant benefits from foster care placement in terms of these outcomes appear unlikely for children at the margin of foster care. . . .

## Family Preservation Can Be More Beneficial than Foster Care

With the child welfare system affecting so many children who appear to be at high risk of poor life outcomes, it would be useful to know whether abused children benefit from being removed from their families. The analysis here uses the effective randomization of abuse investigators, who differ somewhat in their tendency to have children placed in foster care, to estimate causal effects of placement on longer-term outcomes. Children assigned to investigators with higher removal rates are more likely to be placed in foster care themselves, and they are found to have higher delinquency rates, along with some evidence of higher teen birth rates and lower earnings. . . .

The estimates suggest that large gains from foster care placement are unlikely for this group of children at the margin of placement, at least for the outcomes studied here.

When interpreting the results, three main caveats should be kept in mind. First, the sample consists of school-age welfare recipients investigated in Illinois. In addition, the negative effects in terms of delinquency and teen motherhood are found in the 10–15 age group where most of the data reside. Future work will consider younger children as they become at risk for these adolescent and young-adult outcomes. In addition, Illinois is a large urban state where placement of children with family members is more popular than the nation as a whole.

Second, the results consider a group on the margin of placement. While this speaks directly to the policy question of whether we should place greater emphasis on family preservation or child protection, it does not attempt to measure the benefit of placement for children in such danger that all investigators would agree the child should be placed.

Last, the outcomes studied here may relate to child well-being as an adolescent, though they may not reflect the potential prevention of serious child abuse in extreme cases. To the extent that the children on the margin of placement are less likely to suffer from the most serious abuse, this may be less of a concern. Still, child welfare agencies may be willing to trade off higher delinquency, teen motherhood, and unemployment rates for slightly lower levels of serious abuse.

# 5

# Foster Children Still Need Support as They Reach Adulthood

***Toni Naccarato and Liliana Hernández***

*Toni Naccarato is an assistant professor at State University of New York (SUNY) Albany's School of Social Welfare. Liliana Hernández is a student in the master's program of social work and public policy at SUNY Albany.*

*Independent Living Skills programs are designed to assist teens who are aging out of government-sponsored child welfare programs. In practice, however, these programs do not take into account diverse circumstances and needs of individuals who are facing inevitable discharge from the system when they reach a certain age. These programs' shortcomings may be due to a lack of oversight because without close evaluation, these expensive programs cannot be held accountable for effectively assisting teenagers who depend on the support for their eventual self-sustenance.*

Each year approximately 20,000 teenagers leave the child welfare system. They do so via emancipation, which simply means that they have reached the state's age of adulthood and are being cut off from foster care with no further aid. Most teenagers in this situation have spent an average of two and a half years in foster care living with relatives or foster parents or in group homes. Since half of all foster children are

Toni Naccarato and Liliana Hernández, "Kicking Kids Out of Foster Care: A Federal Program to Help Young People Falls Short," *ColorLines*, vol. 11, July/August 2008, pp. 14–15. 

kids of color, they are also overrepresented among those who are kicked out of the system. Overnight, they are expected to support themselves and live as adults, covering their own costs for housing, food, transportation and other basic necessities.

Eighteen-year-old Domonica is one of these young people. She was placed in foster care at birth because of her mother's drug addiction, and over the course of her short life, she has lived in 12 foster homes and two group homes in Schenectady County, New York. At the age of 15, while living in a group home, Domonica gave birth to a little girl who is now 3 years old. Unlike most foster youth, Domonica will be staying in foster care until she turns 21. In New York State, foster youth can remain in care until this age, but in most states, young people are forced out of foster care when they graduate from high school or turn 18. By the age of 18, many foster youth are also weary of the system, and they sign themselves out, often times at their own peril. Very few foster kids leave the child welfare system with a high school diploma, and even fewer attend college. Applying to college, meeting scholarship deadlines, writing essays and getting a resume in order are all stressful enough for high school students living in their own homes.

---

*The vast majority of foster children are cut off from government aid at the age of 18 and are suddenly expected to furnish themselves with housing, employment, transportation and job skills.*

---

Domonica knows this firsthand, "How are foster youth supposed to stay on top of this when in the back of their head, they know they'll be discharged at age 18?" she wonders. She will be attending college . . . and attributes this to her own determination—her caseworkers didn't offer much encouragement. "They just ignored it," she says. "They didn't even ask me what I wanted. It was all my decision." Domonica and her daughter live . . . with a foster mother who is supportive, but she fears that when she turns 21 and is discharged from foster care, she won't be able to make ends meet.

## Independent Living Skills Programs Fall Short

The federal government makes an effort to prepare young people for leaving foster care. The program, Independent Living Skills, is intended to provide foster youth with adult living skills beginning at the age of 16 until the age of 18 (21 in some states). The program, which was started in 1985 and is currently funded at $140 million annually, looks workable on the surface, but there are two major problems.

First, the vast majority of foster children are cut off from government aid at the age of 18 and are suddenly expected to furnish themselves with housing, employment, transportation and job skills—vital training that the program does not always address. The program allows states to extend Medicaid eligibility until the age of 21 and has made some increases in housing resources. These have not been clearly defined and so implementation falls short. And it does little to ensure that these young adults who have had extremely traumatic backgrounds and possess little, if any, familial and financial resources, are ready to be on their own.

The second problem with the Independent Living Skills Program is that there is very little in the area of evaluation and outcome-based studies that measure its effectiveness. In 1999, the Government Accountability Office [GAO] actually released a report that was entitled *Foster Care: Effectiveness of Independent Living Skills Services Unknown*. There are still no standard measures of how states report the program interventions and the number of young people whom the program serves.

Domonica took some Independent Living classes when she was 15 and lived in a group home. "One was about money management, about how to use a checkbook, but they didn't really teach you how to productively spend your money," she says. "It was more just how to keep track of it. I think more classes on how to spend your money wisely would be helpful, because sometimes I just end up buying my baby things that make her look cute, but maybe that's not what she needs."

She also echoes a reality that many foster youth face. "It's harder in a group home to learn basics like cooking and cleaning," she says. "They try to teach you life skills, but in a foster home it's easier to learn about cooking." In group homes, the staff often takes on the responsibility for cooking. "But in some ways, you are forced to be more independent in a group home, because they are not always looking after you," Domonica says. "It's your responsibility to wake up in the morning and go to school or work."

*It is equally an abuse to toss out foster youth without any skills, money or education . . . and then blame the young people if they cannot make a success of their lives.*

## Funds Should Be Used for Real Needs

Young people who grow up in foster care are at a higher risk of homelessness, incarceration and dropping out of high school, and are in need of treatment for substance abuse and mental health issues. It is incumbent on federal and state officials to design programs that include financial assistance for newly emancipated youth, perhaps as much as $5,000 per child, beyond the cutoff age of 18. This money could cover necessities like shelter, food and clothing. More importantly, however, there needs to be a standardized evaluation of all social programs that serve this foster care population. If research proves that this program works, then participation should be encouraged with outreach and educational efforts. Further, why not make all state's Independent Living programs serve youth until the age of 23? On the other hand, if research proves that the program is not effective, then it might be wise to eliminate the program and offer a cash grant for youth upon leaving the system.

Some children end up in foster care because of child abuse. But it is equally an abuse to toss out foster youth without any skills, money or education and to do so with a taxpayer-funded program that we don't know anything about—and then blame the young people if they cannot make a success of their lives.

6

# Kinship Care Benefits Foster Children

***Marlene Busko***

*Marlene Busko is a staff journalist for the Medscape Psychiatry and Mental Health Web site.*

*The National Survey of Child and Adolescent Well-Being was conducted by the U.S. Department of Health and Human Services to address three major issues: 1. the children and families who come into contact with the child welfare system; 2. the interactions of children and families while in the child welfare system; and 3. the short- and long-term effects for these children and families. Results of the study suggest that children who can be placed in the care of relatives rather than unfamiliar foster parents are less likely to have behavior problems and more likely to find stability and permanency in their residency.*

A national US survey showed that children who were maltreated by their parents and sent to live with relatives (kinship care) had better 3-year behavioral outcomes than those placed in foster care.

The findings come from a sample of 1309 maltreated children who were placed into kinship and foster care and who participated in the National Survey of Child and Adolescent Well-Being (NSCAW).

"When kinship care is a realistic option and appropriate safeguards have been met, children in kinship care might have

Marlene Busko, "Maltreated Children Placed in Kinship vs. Foster Care May Have Fewer Behavioral Problems," *Medscape Medical News*, June 6, 2008. Reproduced by permission. www.medscape.com.

an advantage over children in foster care in achieving permanency and improved well-being, albeit with the recognition that their needs will remain great, exceeding those of children who have not experienced child maltreatment," the researchers, led by David M. Rubin, MD, from Children's Hospital of Philadelphia, in Pennsylvania, write.

The study is published in the June [2008] issue of the *Archives of Pediatrics & Adolescent Medicine.*

*The growth in kinship care is the result of sustained effort to improve residence permanency of children.*

## More Abused Children Being Placed with Family Members

The 2005 US census report revealed that more than 2.5 million children were living with a relative caregiver other than a birth parent, which is a 55% increase from 15 years earlier, the authors write. Children are placed in out-of-home care most often as a result of child abuse or neglect, they add.

The growth in kinship care is the result of sustained effort to improve residence permanency of children since the Adoption and Safe Families Act of 1997, they continue, noting that a large body of evidence shows that kinship care generally results in a more permanent placement than foster care. On the other hand, some evidence raises concerns that, with kinship care, children may have greater access to abusive parents and face additional hardships, since their caregivers are generally older, poorer, and have more mental health problems than foster caregivers.

This prospective cohort study aimed to use NSCAW findings—which looked at children at baseline and at 18 and 36 months after placement—to estimate the association between placement into kinship care and the likelihood of behavioral problems after out-of-home care.

The primary outcome was the child's behavioral well-being at 18 and 36 months, as measured by the Child Behavior Checklist (CBCL) caregiver-reported survey.

*If all children had been assigned to only foster care, the estimate of behavior problems at 36 months was 46%, vs. 32% if they had all been placed in early kinship care.*

At baseline, of the 1309 children who met the study criteria, 28% were younger than 2 years old, 50% were 2 to 10 years old, and 22% were older than 10 years old.

The sample comprised:

- 599 children who entered kinship care within 1 month of placement into out-of-home care (early kinship care).
- 584 children who entered and remained in foster care (foster care).
- 126 children who entered kinship care after more than 1 month in foster care (late kinship care).

## Study Supports Kinship Placement

Children in the early-kinship-care group had a lower marginal probability of behavioral problems at 36 months than children in the other 2 groups. If all children had been assigned to only foster care, the estimate of behavior problems at 36 months was 46%, vs. 32% if they had all been placed in early kinship care.

Compared with children in the other 2 groups, children in early kinship care were less likely to experience placement instability.

"While this study provides evidence to encourage the placement of children with willing and available kin, we urge caution in interpreting the findings for 3 reasons," the group writes. First, the survey did not collect sufficient information to determine whether children placed in foster care had acceptable, safe alternatives in their own families. Second, kin caregivers might have been less likely to report behavioral problems among children in their care. Third, the results are not the product of a randomized study. In addition, there are concerns about generalizability because the data likely missed temporary, informal kinship arrangements.

Nevertheless, "this finding supports efforts to maximize placement of children with willing and available kin when they enter out-of-home care," they conclude.

## Need to Expand Resources for Kinship Guardians

"The study by Rubin et al. is one of the best ever performed on the outcomes of kinship care," Richard P. Barth, PhD, from the School of Social Work at the University of Maryland, in Baltimore, writes in an accompanying editorial. He cautions, however, that "being in kinship care and having fewer behavior problems likely comprise a relationship that is too complicated to be thought of as being causal and one-way."

The study, however, does broadly imply that child welfare workers should endeavor to reduce placement moves for all children, he adds.

"The recommendations of the authors to expand the resources given to kinship providers with a national kinship guardianship program and to endeavor to more expeditiously notify kin and place children into kinship care deserve underscoring," Dr. Barth notes, adding that these are low-cost strategies that deserve implementation, given the evidence that children prefer to be placed with relatives and their behavioral outcomes appear to be better.

7

# Group Homes Help At-Risk Youth

***Michael C. Farley***

*Michael C. Farley is a representative of the Virginia Coalition of Private Provider Associations and the executive director of Elk Hill Farm, a youth group home.*

*The Comprehensive Services Act for At-Risk Youth and Families (CSA) provides funding and services for high-risk youth in the state of Virginia. Among those funded services are residential facilities that house and educate multiple children who would otherwise be in foster care or other child welfare services. These residential programs pay special attention to children's emotional, behavioral, and learning problems, and the adults who care for them become like surrogate parents. Agents of group homes may continue to work for children's reunification or adoption, or they may invest in the children's education and life skills training for when they become independent.*

Elk Hill Farm was established in 1970 serving 6 boys. During the past 37 years our organization has grown to 4 sites and 7 programs throughout central Virginia. Last year [2006] we served 260 children and their families through a variety of programs; in home community outreach, our two day schools, our two group homes, our residential school, an aftercare program and a therapeutic academic summer camp—serving

Michael C. Farley, The Hanger Commission, Richmond, VA: Virginia Coalition of Private Provider Associations (VCOPPA), 2007. 

7-10-year-old inner city Richmond kids. At the request of Fluvanna County, next month we will be opening a group home for 8 young women, Elk Hill—Spring Garden, located in Bremo Bluff. Elk Hill's programs are licensed by the Departments of Education and Social Services. Our schools are fully accredited by the Virginia Council for Private Education and the Virginia Association of Independent Specialized Education Facilities.

Today I am also representing the Virginia Coalition of Private Provider Associations—VCOPPA. Private providers under the VCOPPA umbrella serve thousands of children and their families through an array of programs ranging from adoption to in home to foster care to psychiatric services. . . .

---

*The structure, treatment, experiences and education provided by these residential programs provide a core foundation for a child to build upon.*

---

## Programs Help At-Risk Children in Virginia

Since the inception of CSA [Child Services Act] an array of programs for at-risk children has been developed across the Commonwealth of Virginia. Important components of this mosaic of services are the residential programs. These programs range from small 4–8 bed group homes to larger psychiatric locked facilities. In-between are a myriad of programs including residential schools and programs serving specific challenges such as substance abuse and sexual offenders. The structure, treatment, experiences and education provided by these residential programs provide a core foundation for a child to build upon.

The CSA concept of a continuum of services from least restrictive (less costly) to more restrictive (more costly) is often the way in which the referral sequence plays out. Many of the boys referred to Elk Hill's residential school have had multiple failed placements prior to arriving on our campus. This practice has resulted in residential placements often times being the final intervention—the last resort—rather than a timely appropriate placement based on the needs of the child and the family.

VCOPPA applauds the . . . For Keeps Initiative. Children deserve permanency. They deserve good schools and after school programs. They deserve to grow up in functional families and functional safe neighborhoods. Unfortunately, the majority of the children served in many residential programs often come from just the opposite. They come from dysfunctional families and/or cultures and/or neighborhoods. Often times, the dysfunction has become literally toxic.

## Challenges for At-Risk Youth

The kids we work with have emotional, behavioral and learning problems, often times as a result of abuse from the hands of those adults entrusted to care for them. They don't trust adults. Our most important responsibilities are to provide a safe environment for a child to grow and to surround these children with reliable caring adults. It often takes a significant period of time before a child realizes that there are adults who can be trusted and counted upon.

---

*In these [independent living] programs the boys can finish high school, attend college, attain employment and work through a curriculum designed to foster independence.*

---

Children do deserve permanency. At Elk Hill we strive for family reunification—whenever it is possible. Our counselors work with moms, dads, grandparents, aunts, uncles, siblings, extended family and foster families on our campus and in their homes to pave the way for a sense of permanency in the child's life. However, there are situations where there are no viable family options. We then work with the child's social worker to develop an alternative permanency plan, which might include adoption or foster care. For older adolescents we try to step the child down to one of our independent living programs—group homes—one in Richmond and one in Charlottesville. In these programs the boys can finish high school, attend college, attain employment and work through a curriculum designed to foster independence.

It is difficult to separate out the behavioral, emotional and educational challenges our kids face. With success in school often times behaviors improve as well as attitudes and vise versa. Most of our kids come into our residential school 2–3 grade levels behind. Their reading levels are—often times—several grade levels behind. Through individual instruction and small class teacher/pupil ratios our kids can increase up to 3 grade levels in one year. Educational progress and success is perhaps the biggest key to these kids becoming responsible adults. Our education does not stop at the classroom. Elk Hill's Education for Employment program provides direction for the transition of our students to the workforce. The program provides students with career exploration, work experience and community service learning.

The challenges that face our kids have often developed over years. The fix is not quick, easy or cheap. Our residential school program costs $253 a day. . . . We subsidize all of our programs through private donations to keep the costs down. We also offer private scholarships to kids whose public funds have dried up and to kids who don't qualify for public funds—those non-mandated children. In 2006 we provided forty-three full and partial scholarships. Our summer academic camp and our Education for Employment program are both privately funded.

## Success Rate

We have followed up on our kids over years. Back in 1984 two professors . . . developed an instrument to measure our kids' success—the Success Rate Index. Their instrument takes a look at the time our kids were doing well after leaving our residential program (defined as living in a less restricted environment) vs. time they are not doing so well (more restrictive environment). Every five years we try to contact as many former students as possible. Last year [2006] we reconnected with 209 boys who had left our residential school in the past 5 years. It's a snapshot but it does provide a look at what has happened to our kids since they left the program. Over eighty percent of their time was spent in less restrictive living situations.

There are many outstanding residential programs in the Commonwealth [of Virginia]. Some are represented here today in the audience. There are programs that send all of their graduates to college. Others provide ongoing assistance well into the child's adult life. These programs also become part of the child's permanence. The adults in these programs become the child's surrogate family. The experience and growth many of these children have in these programs remain with them for a lifetime.

I have been fortune to have spent the past 27 years working at Elk Hill. During those 27 years, I have witnessed hundreds of lives transformed from despair to hopefulness. Returning to the US from the Peace Corps in Africa in 1980, I thought I would never find an experience as rewarding and fulfilling as my Peace Corps days. I was wrong.

# 8

# Group Homes Increase the Risk of Delinquency for Foster Children

***Craig Chamberlain***

*Craig Chamberlain is news editor for the News Bureau at the University of Illinois at Urbana-Champaign.*

*A study of the Los Angeles area child welfare system gives particular attention to the relationship between children's group home residence and the incidence of arrest. According to statistical evidence, children in group homes are 2.5 times more likely than children in foster homes to be arrested. The researchers involved in the study are concerned for all children dependent on protective services who enter the juvenile justice system because their resources and options are even further limited.*

Group homes are generally the placement of last resort for children in foster care, and also one of the most expensive options for state child-welfare agencies.

It appears that group homes also play a significant role in pushing the children they serve toward the juvenile-justice system, according to a new study in Los Angeles County, led by a University of Illinois professor.

## Group Home Youths Are Often Arrested

"Our results found that kids (mostly adolescents) who enter group home placements are about two-and-a-half times more likely to enter the juvenile-justice system relative to similar

Craig Chamberlain, "Group Homes Appear to Double Delinquency Risk for Foster Kids, Study Says," News Bureau: University of Illinois at Urbana-Champaign, February 28, 2008. Reproduced by permission. www.news.uiuc.edu.

kids, with similar backgrounds, who are served in foster-home settings," says Joseph Ryan, a professor in the Children and Family Research Center (CFRC), part of the university's School of Social work.

What is more, Ryan said, the group-home effect on delinquency appears to be fairly immediate. "The vast majority of (first-time) arrests occur while the adolescent is actually under the supervision of the group home," rather than months or years after they leave, he said.

*Keeping foster youth out of the juvenile-justice system is especially important because they have fewer options once there.*

Keeping foster youth out of the juvenile-justice system is especially important because they have fewer options once there, Ryan said. "We know once child-welfare youth are in the juvenile-justice system, they're less likely to get probation and more likely to get pushed deeper into the juvenile-justice system," he said.

Another concern grows from the fact that African Americans are overrepresented in the child-welfare system, and in group homes specifically, Ryan said. The group-home effect therefore might be contributing to the even greater overrepresentation of African Americans in the juvenile-justice system, as well as in prisons, he said. . . .

The study and its conclusions were made possible by a unique data-sharing agreement that gave researchers access to both child-welfare and juvenile-justice records in Los Angeles County, Ryan said. They were able to track individuals in their movements through both systems, and see connections between the two, he said.

Previous research has shown a connection between foster care and delinquency and other negative outcomes—some of that research even suggesting that children might be better off staying in troubled homes rather than going into foster care, Ryan said. "Those findings might lead one to erroneously believe that all child-welfare placements are problematic, and perhaps equally problematic," he said.

The study of Los Angeles County, he said, shows that different kinds of placements can have dramatically different effects.

## Implementing the Study

As a starting point for the study, researchers had access to administrative records for all children and families involved with the Department of Children and Family Services and the Department of Probation in Los Angeles County, in both cases for the period between 2001 and 2005. From those records, they compiled a sample of all the children between the ages of 7 and 16 who had been placed outside their own home by child welfare at least once.

---

*Children and adolescents placed in group homes . . . have generally been through more placements, are slightly older, and have more characteristics often associated with delinquency.*

---

Children and adolescents placed in group homes, compared with those placed only in foster care family settings, have generally been through more placements, are slightly older, and have more characteristics often associated with delinquency, Ryan said. The authors used econometric methods, known as propensity score matching, to help disentangle the effect of those individual characteristics from the effect associated with group-home placement, he said.

By way of this method, they matched 4,113 youth who had been in group homes with 4,113 with similar characteristics who had only been served in foster family home placements. Twenty percent of the group-home sample experienced at least one arrest, as compared with 8 percent of the matched foster-care sample.

## Both the Number and Type of Offenses Are Affected

Ryan said he was surprised by the size of the group-home effect, even after controlling for individual differences. He was also surprised by the differences that emerged with regard to the type of offending. Group-home youth were significantly more likely to be arrested for violent and threat-related offenses.

As to why children in group-home settings are more likely to experience arrests and enter the juvenile-justice system, Ryan said he sees two promising areas for research.

One involves the possibility of "peer contagion," in which deviant adolescents influence one another to become more delinquent than they otherwise would have been. Related, he said, is the common practice of mixing delinquent and non-delinquent youth in congregate or group-home settings.

The other area involves looking at whether group-home policies or procedures cause staff to more readily contact law enforcement in given situations and whether those might contribute to the likelihood of arrest for a given behavior.

"It does raise the question of whether there is a lower threshold in group settings versus other foster-home settings," Ryan said. "Are staff more likely to engage law enforcement to resolve physical and threat-related conflict, which then sets off a chain of negative events?"

# 9

# White Families May Not Be the Best Choice for Adopting Black Children

***David Crary***

*David Crary writes for the* Chicago Citizen, *a newspaper dedicated to the rights of African-American youth.*

*In the child welfare community, an ongoing debate circles around the care of minority children in foster care. The concern is that white families may not be sensitive to the cultural differences between the races when they adopt black children. The crux of the problem is the disproportionately high numbers of black children in the foster care system. Leading child welfare groups support legislation that encourages adoption of black children by black families, but training programs do exist that work to prepare white parents to care for minority children with a sensitive and realistic approach.*

Several leading child welfare groups . . . urged an overhaul of federal laws dealing with transracial adoption, arguing that black children in foster care are ill-served by a "color-blind" approach meant to encourage their adoption by white families.

Recommendations for major changes in the much-debated policy were outlined in a report by the Evan B. Donaldson Adoption Institute.

David Crary, "Major Changes Urged in Transracial Adoption," *Chicago Citizen*, vol. 43, May 28, 2008, p. 11. 

"Color consciousness—not 'color blindness'—should help to shape policy development," the report said.

Groups endorsing its proposals included the North American Council on Adoptable Children, the Child Welfare League of America, the Dave Thomas Foundation for Adoption and the National Association of Black Social Workers.

## The Multi-Ethnic Placement Act

At issue is the 1994 Multi-Ethnic Placement Act—and revisions made to it in 1996—governing the adoption of children from foster care.

One part of the law directs state agencies to recruit more adoptive parents of the same race as the children. The new report says this provision hasn't been adequately enforced and calls for better funded efforts to recruit minority parents.

---

*All children deserve to be raised in families that respect their cultural heritage.*

---

The more contentious part of the legislation prohibits race from being taken into consideration in most decisions about adoption from foster care. For example, white parents seeking to adopt a black child cannot be required to undergo race-oriented training that differs in any way from training that all prospective adoptive parents receive.

A key recommendation in the new report calls for amending the law so race could be considered as a factor in selecting parents for children from foster care. The change also would allow race-oriented pre-adoption training.

"We tried to assess what was working and what wasn't, and came to the conclusion that preparing parents who adopt transracially benefits everyone, especially the children," said Adam Pertman, the Donaldson Institute's executive director.

"The view that we can be color-blind is a wonderful, idealistic perspective, but we don't live there," Pertman said. "If we want to do the best for the kids, we have to look at their realities."

## High Number of Black Children in Foster Care

At the heart of the debate is the fact that the foster care system has a disproportionately high number of black children, and on average they languish there nine months longer than white children before moving to permanent homes. The latest federal figures showed 32 percent of the 510,000 children in foster care were black in 2006, compared to 15 percent of all U.S. children.

Of the black children adopted out of foster care, about 20 percent are adopted by white families. The Donaldson report said current federal law, by stressing color blindness, deters child welfare agencies from assessing families' readiness to adopt transracially or preparing them for the distinctive challenges they might face.

"There is a higher rate of problems in minority foster children adopted transracially than in-race," said the report. "All children deserve to be raised in families that respect their cultural heritage."

Pertman stressed that his institute and its allies were not opposed to transracial adoption.

"We want to see more kids in foster care get permanent homes, and we want to see the parents who raise those children be prepared to do so," he said.

## Color Blindness

Professor Elizabeth Bartholet, who directs the Child Advocacy Program at Harvard Law School, believes the concept of striving for color blindness is sound. She foresees problems if race once again becomes a key determinant.

"Giving social workers the chance to do that produced very rigid race matching," she said, referring to pre-1994 policies. "That's one of the reasons to say race can't be used at all—there's no other way to be sure it doesn't become the overwhelming factor."

Current policy allows standardized pre-adoption training, but wisely prohibits specific screening for parents seeking to adopt transracially, Bartholet said.

"What cannot be done is have a pass/fail test that turns on whether you give the politically correct answers," she said. "If social workers are allowed to use training to determine who can adopt, there's lots of experience showing they abuse that power."

She also questioned whether attempts to boost minority recruitment would succeed.

"Black people are significantly poorer than white people and less likely to be in a position to come forward," Bartholet said. "Recruitment efforts bump up against that fact."

---

*Too many white adoptive parents . . . underestimate the enduring presence of racism in America and don't get training that would help them raise a black child.*

---

## White Adoptive Parents Don't Understand Racism

The Donaldson recommendations were embraced as "long overdue" by Michelle Johnson, a black woman raised by white adoptive parents near Minneapolis. Johnson now works on child-welfare matters for the court system there.

Her parents "were not the norm," she said. "They were exceptional in what they did for me . . . They were very humble in what they didn't know. There was lots of communication."

Too many white adoptive parents, she said, underestimate the enduring presence of racism in America and don't get training that would help them raise a black child.

"As a social worker who used to place children, I know very few families are ready to do this," Johnson said. "When families fail to realize they need assistance, it's dangerous."

Regarding recruitment, Johnson said child welfare agencies should strive to find permanent homes for black children among their extended families before placing them in foster care.

## Perfect Matches Are Hard to Find

John Mould and Margaret Gelger, an Ambler, Pa., couple, have two white biological children and five black adopted children, now aged 15 to 23. Mould said transracial adoption is unquestionably challenging, but he worries about any changes that might make training and screening requirements too rigid.

"There are so many kids who need homes," Mould said. "The idea of trying to find the perfect matches—you're not going to find them."

His adopted children have encountered some difficulties over the years, Mould said, but he believes they've developed resiliency and maturity as a result.

His youngest son, Eric Jones, 15, said the family's makeup sometimes complicates his life, but he's convinced that transracial adoption can succeed.

"White or black doesn't matter," he said. "What counts is whether the parents are ready to take responsibility."

# 10

# Race Should Not Be a Consideration When Adopting a Child

***Curtis L. Ivery***

*Curtis L. Ivery is chancellor of the Wayne County Community College District in Michigan.*

*Race should not be considered when adopting black children because there are more children in need of homes than there are available parents. Black children waiting for adoption by a black family may never have the chance to live in a permanent home unless the pool of available parents is expanded. It is more important for a black child to have a safe, permanent home with a white family than to endure an unsafe situation with foster care placement. Furthermore, multiracial and transracial adoptions have occurred successfully for years, providing suitable permanent homes for children of all backgrounds.*

There is nothing more painful than to contemplate what lies ahead for the thousands of young Black children wasting away in foster homes, victims of the worst mental and physical abuse and neglect any society can impose on them. Many are born to drug and alcohol addicts, which relegate them to a life of mental retardation, attention deficit disorders, language problems and all sorts of poor social skills.

These unfortunate souls are bounced between foster families for their entire childhood, a punishing life. They con-

Curtis L. Ivery, "Foster Care, In Focus," *Michigan Chronicle*, vol. 70, August 28, 2007, p. A5. 

stantly yearn for and cry out for loving and protective families that they rarely find. Just thinking about them is enough to bring tears to your eyes. That's why we don't want to be reminded of the children we would rather forget.

*Michigan ranks close to the national numbers with 56.9 [percent] of the children in [state-supported] care being Black, Hispanic or American-Indian.*

With that disconcerting portrait as a backdrop, I cringed as I read newspaper accounts that referenced the most recent Kids Count in Michigan report that found that more than 28,690 Michigan children spent some time in foster care during 2004. This statistic has doubled during the last decade with a disproportionate number who were removed from homes and placed in state-supported care being children of color. Michigan ranks close to the national numbers with 56.9 [percent] of the children in care being Black, Hispanic or American-Indian (while only comprising 42 percent of the total number of children in the state).

What was missing from the newspaper articles that did address "lost Black children" in foster care was one sympathetic word from those who purport to care about Black advancement, if only to declare "What a shame."

## More Children Need Homes

My intent here is to become an advocate for poorly reared often ill-treated and lowly regarding Black children without a permanent address. Let me begin by saying I'm convinced there are legitimate reasons for the state to remove children from dysfunctional homes and parents. Seventy percent of those in foster care were reported as neglected, 20.1 percent were physically abused and 5.5 percent were sexually abused. This doesn't even begin to address babies exposed to heroin and cocaine in the womb who never have a chance. Often born prematurely, they require expensive, intensive care from day one. Typically irritable and extremely difficult to nurture, these infants need special medical help as well as attention for developmental problems that often do not surface until age two or three. Since addicted parents can't be expected to maintain a habit and the minimum amount of care for children at the same time, more than half of these kids end up in state-supported care. The rest are shuttled off to grandparents or other family members.

Arguably the greater tragedy would be to leave drug addicted infants and children with biological parents who are caught up in addiction. Those who are abandoned or removed from their homes may be the fortunate ones.

The problem is that thousands end up in a mismanaged and overcrowded foster care system while courts and social workers try to decide if adoption is right for them. Only 2,622 children in Michigan were legally adopted in 2004. It is not uncommon for kids to be moved from one dysfunctional family to another by being matched with foster parents who are in the child care business only for the money. Some children become involved with the criminal justice system from the turmoil and confusion of neglect and prolonged foster care. Others have long-term social, emotional and physical scars from which they never recover and never reach their potential.

## Some Children Can't Be Adopted

What's even worse is that these children may be too abused, too damaged, too handicapped and too troubled to be marketable for adoption. There is a larger pool of potentially adoptable babies and waiting children than at any time in our history. But there aren't enough foster parents or adoptive families to handle the increase in abused and neglected children. Still, drug addicted babies are placed with parents who don't want a mentally or physically impaired child where the abuse continues. Few are adopted.

Granted, these circumstances make it difficult for our adoption system to bring childless couples and needy children together. But the process is further complicated by too much red tape and too many tangled rules, regulations and procedures. More than 7,152 Michigan youth are available for adoption. However, since many social agencies are compensated for each child in foster care, they have no incentive to expedite the movement of children through the system and into waiting families. Some of those who control the selection and placement process apply inappropriate standards in evaluating the qualifications of families. A few years back, the color of a prospective parent's skin determined what color baby you were eligible for. Race weighed heavily in the evaluation of the qualifications and fitness of foster parents.

*Skin tone has long been an inappropriate standard on which to evaluate the qualifications of families of any color to love and to care for and raise children.*

## Legislation Does Not Prevent Transracial Adoptions

There is no federal or state law prohibiting transracial adoptions. Neither are there policy restrictions on transracial foster parent placement. Yet, Black social work organizations and national advocacy groups denounced interracial adoptions out of a perceived fear that Black children would somehow lose their sense of racial pride, be separated from their culture and suffer an identity crisis if placed in another social and economic environment. In turn, adoption agencies were pressured into steering White families away from Black children.

I'm not sure how much this is practiced today. What I do know is that hundreds of Black, brown, light and dark skinned children are born to multiracial parents. Thousands of White and Black Americans routinely adopt Asian children without challenge or stigma. So skin tone has long been an inappropriate standard on which to evaluate the qualifications of families of any color to love and to care for and raise children.

There are a decreasing number of willing, qualified, drug-free financially able White and Black parents to care for the kids who are born into desperate situations. I am concerned that children who think they are alone and unwanted grow into adults who harbor frustration and anger detrimental to the communities in which they live. We should all be concerned that thousands of young people are being cast out into our neighborhoods as a result of "aging out" of the system with little preparation, skills or ability to support or sustain themselves—but they will by whatever means necessary. Thus, we are presented with a moral dilemma that raises questions about our strength and our resolve as a strong, caring community that places a high priority on our children. It is time for us to take a stand and do what is right. Let's make sure that our kids do count.

# 11

# The Indian Child Welfare Act Is Needed to Preserve American Indian Culture

***Heidi Kiiwetinepinesiik Stark and Kekek Jason Todd Stark***

*Heidi Kiiwetinepinesiik Stark received her BA in American Indian Studies at the University of Minnesota. Kekek Jason Todd Stark served as an Indian Child Welfare Act Court Monitor for the Minneapolis American Indian Center.*

*Following the removal of large numbers of American Indian children from their homes, American Indian leaders pressed for the passage of legislation that would protect their children and the future of their culture. The Indian Child Welfare Act places more power for unique child welfare decisions with tribal court judges, who have the cultural background needed to identify proper placement for American Indian children. This legislation also looks out for the long-term survival of American Indian tribes when fewer youths leave them behind; placements within the reservations preserve the future generations.*

## The Indian Child Welfare Act Is Needed to Preserve American Indian Culture

James Waldram, in *The Way of the Pipe*, recounts the story of an eagle who thought he was a chicken. As the story goes, one day a farmer found a wounded eagle and placed him out in the chickens' coop to recover. This eagle began mimicking the

Heidi Kiiwetinepinesiik Stark and Kekek Jason Todd Stark, "Flying the Coop: Historical and Procedural Elements of the Indian Child Welfare Act," *Outsiders Within: Writing on Transracial Adoption*, eds. Jane Jeong Trenka, Julia Chinyere Oparah, and Sun Yung Shin. South End Press, 2006. 

chickens to survive in his new environment. He ate like the chickens, slept like the chickens, and adopted the behavior of the chickens. Then one day an Indian man came by the farm and saw this eagle who thought he was a chicken.

So he said, "What's that eagle doing there in the chicken coop?" The farmer said, "Well, I found it in the ditch, mended its wing and put him in there. The eagle can fly out any time. Its wing is healed. He just thinks he's a chicken I guess."

The farmer agreed to let this Indian man take the eagle out of the coop, but the eagle remained docile. He just kept bobbing his head like a chicken. The eagle no longer understood who he was, no longer identified as an eagle and appreciated the gifts that came with that identity. So the Indian took the bird to the mountain and said, "You have to know who you are and what you stand for." The eagle started to flex his wings. His keen eyesight started to return, and the strength in him started to come back. The eagle flew and soared and everything came back to him, who he was and that he wasn't a chicken. He gained everything he'd lost because of where he was placed.

---

*[American Indian children's] removal from their homes and placement outside their tribal communities has led to a loss of identity.*

---

Many American Indian children are in a situation that parallels this story. Their removal from their homes and placement outside their tribal communities has led to a loss of identity. They often risk becoming eagles that behave like chickens. Tribal nations have struggled against state, county, and local agencies, attempts to remove their children and place them in non-Indian homes, the symbolic chicken coop. Their fight to limit the destructive results of this mass removal led to the Indian Child Welfare Act (ICWA).

American Indian children accounted for 3.1 percent of the total population of children cared for out of their homes, even though they were less than 1 percent of the total child population in the 1950s and '60s. Therefore American Indian children were in out-of-home placement at a rate of 3.6 times greater than the rate for non-Indian children.

*Local and state agencies removed Indian children applying determinants that ignored the traumatic effects this forceful removal was having.*

## A Need for the ICWA

Doubts about the capacity of American Indian families to raise their children continued long after the boarding school era. State agencies argued that removal was in the best interest of many American Indian children, which resulted in "as many as 25 to 35 percent of the Indian children in some states [who] were removed from their homes and placed in non-Indian homes by state-courts, welfare agencies, and private adoption agencies" before the passage of the Indian Child Welfare act in 1978. Congress also found that countrywide, Indian children were placed in foster care or in adoptive homes at 5 times the rate of non-Indian children, while in Montana, foster care placement for Indian children was at least 13 times greater than for non-Indian children; in South Dakota, adoptions of American Indian children accounted for 40 percent of all adoptions made by the state's Department of Public Welfare between 1967 and 1978, even though they were only 7 percent of the juvenile population; in Washington, the Indian adoption rate was 19 times greater and the foster care rate was 10 times greater; and in Wisconsin, Indian children ran the risk of being separated from their parents at a rate nearly 1600 percent greater than non-Indian children. . . .

The removal of Native children would lead to far more serious problems than adoptive agencies and local/state agencies anticipated. Local and state agencies removed Indian children applying determinants that ignored the traumatic effects this forceful removal was having. Congress recognized the concerns raised by American Indian activists and leaders during a 1978 hearing. The Subcommittee on Indian Affairs declared that:

> The separation of Indian children from their natural parents, especially their placement in institutions or homes, which do not meet their special needs, is socially and culturally undesirable. For the child, such separation can cause a loss of identity and self-esteem, and contributes directly to the unreasonable high rates among Indian children for dropouts, alcoholism and drug abuse, suicides and crime.

## Transracial Placements Weaken Cultural Identity

Congress also argued that the removal of American Indian children aggravated the conditions that initially gave rise to the break-up of the family, that this perpetuates the continuing cycle of poverty and despair.

These issues have been a concern of Indian child-welfare advocates working to decrease depression, suicide, and alcoholism. At a 1990 conference on the ICWA, presenters Evelyn Blanchard and Irving Berlin discussed the long-term effects of out-of-home placement, presenting findings from a study of 100,000 Indian children in foster placement. . . . Trans-racial placements were proving to have detrimental effects on American Indian children.

In 1968 members of the Devil's Lake Sioux Tribe of North Dakota, concerned with the level of cultural decimation they were facing, approached the Association on American Indian Affairs (AAIA), established in 1923 to "defend the rights of American Indians and Alaskan Natives and to promote social, economic, and civic equality for their communities." The AAIA began work on the issue, bringing awareness and information to public and professional channels while collecting data and testimonials to present to the federal government.

## The Need for Legislation

In an examination of child welfare practices for American Indian children, the Committee on Interior and Insular Affairs in the House of Representatives found that the separation of the children from their families generally occurred when:

1. The natural parent does not understand the nature of the documents or proceedings involved;
2. Neither the child nor the natural parents are represented by counsel or otherwise advised of their rights;
3. The agency officials involved are unfamiliar with, and often disdainful of, Indian culture and society;
4. The conditions that led to the separation are not demonstrably harmful or are remediable or transitory in character; and
5. Responsible tribal authorities are not consulted about or even informed of the non-tribal government actions.

In addition to these concerns, Congress recognized that Tribes were being denied their right to govern their children and be notified of the conditions facing their own people. Thus, a Declaration of Policy was established during hearings for the ICWA stating:

> The Congress hereby declares that it is the policy of this nation, in its fulfillment of its special responsibilities and legal obligations to the American Indian people, to establish standards for the placement of Indian children in foster or adoptive homes which will reflect the unique values of Indian culture, discourage unnecessary placement of Indian children in boarding schools for social rather than educational reasons, assist Indian tribes in the operation of tribal family development programs, and generally promote the stability and security of Indian families.

## ICWA Becomes Law

The ICWA became law on November 8, 1978. In the act, Congress clearly defined "the relationship of the federal government to the tribes, determining that the Federal government has assumed the responsibility for the protection and preservation of Indian tribes and their resources," including their children. The act was passed with two specific goals: It intended to protect individual Indian children and the maintenance of their families while protecting the future existence of the tribe as a sovereign entity because "removal of Indian children from their cultural setting seriously impacts long-term tribal survival and has damaging social and psychological impact on many individual Indian children."

---

*Tribes are flexing their wings, reclaiming and reasserting jurisdiction over American Indian child welfare, and partnering with local, county, and state social welfare systems on behalf of their children.*

---

The Senate Report on the ICWA incorporated the testimony of Louis La Rose, chairman of the Winnebago tribe, before the American Indian Policy Review Commission:

> I think the crudest trick that the white man has ever done to Indian children is to take them into adoption courts, erase all of their records and send them off to some nebulous family that has a contrary value system and that child reaches 16 or 17, he is a little brown child residing in a white community and he goes back to the reservation and he has absolutely no idea who his relatives are, and they effectively make him a nonperson and I think they destroy him.

Jurisdictional provisions are the core of the Indian Child Welfare Act, because the ICWA was written with the acknowledgement that "tribal court judges are more knowledgeable than state court judges about Indian childrearing customs and traditions." The ICWA thus gives exclusive jurisdiction to the tribal court if the child lives on the reservation or is a ward of the court. When the child resides off the reservation, then the child's tribe and the state court have concurrent jurisdiction.

Today, tribes are flexing their wings, reclaiming and reasserting jurisdiction over American Indian child welfare, and partnering with local, county, and state social welfare systems on behalf of their children. As this history is understood and the procedural elements of the ICWA are implemented, Indian children will begin to "fly the coop," remembering that they are "eagles," not "chickens," and recovering what has been lost for generations.

# 12

# Schools Take Steps to Meet the Educational Needs of Foster Children

***Linda Jacobson***

*Linda Jacobson is an assistant editor for* Education Week.

*Academic performance of foster children often lags behind that of average students due to many factors, including developmental problems, transiency, and poverty. Several states are taking part in pilot programs, with federal government support, that work to improve overall cooperation among social workers, foster parents, educators, and individuals, in the interest of the children's educational success. Substandard environments suffer from ill-informed caregivers and resistant educators and administrators, and advocates are pushing for awareness about foster children's special education needs.*

Policy makers from Congress to the state and local levels are sharpening their focus on the educational needs of children in foster care, a population that can exceed 700,000 nationally in the course of a year and which has doubled in the past two decades.

In many cases, their strategies coincide with recommendations outlined in a recent report on California's massive foster-care system: access to preschool for foster children, specialized training for teachers, and making sure child-welfare agencies have educational liaisons.

"A focus on school readiness and school success may not heal all the damage already inflicted early in the lives of foster children, but it can give these children—and many of their peers—the fighting chance they need and deserve to thrive as adults," says the report, released [in May 2008] by the Center for the Future of Teaching and Learning in Santa Cruz, Calif, and Mental Health Advocacy Services, Inc., a Los Angeles-based public-interest law firm.

Among the signs of renewed attention to the educational needs of foster children:

- The reauthorization of the federal Head Start preschool program last fall [2007] lists children in foster care as one of the groups designated to receive priority for enrollment.
- Efforts are under way in Congress to include foster children in the federal McKinney-Vento Act, which is meant to provide school stability, transportation, and other educational services for homeless children.
- A six-state project launched by the National Governors Association [NGA] last month [May 2008] includes improved school performance for foster children as one of its goals in an effort to cut the number of children in foster care by 50 percent in the next 12 years.

---

*Foster-care providers tend to have fewer resources to support learning than do traditional families.*

---

## Added Challenges

Such efforts are intended to help compensate for a range of challenges facing children in foster-care placement.

Foster-care providers tend to have fewer resources to support learning than do traditional families, according to William O'Hare, the coordinator of Kids Count, a project of the Annie E. Casey Foundation, a Baltimore-based philanthropy.

For example, U.S. Census Bureau data show that the average income in foster households is lower than that of traditional homes with children—$56,364, compared with $74,301. In addition; Mr. O'Hare said, foster parents are more likely than traditional parents to be unemployed and have less than a high school education.

At a recent presentation to a Population Association of America conference in New Orleans, where he outlined those statistics, Mr. O'Hare said such factors can have serious drawbacks for the educational success of children in foster care.

Foster families "have fewer human resources and fewer financial resources," he said in a subsequent interview. "It's got to have a negative impact."

The NGA pilot program, which began last month [May 2008], seeks to address some of those issues, even as it aims to bring down the number of children in out-of-home placements.

The association's Center for Best Practices has chosen six states—Arkansas, Florida, Oklahoma, Oregon, Pennsylvania, and South Carolina—to participate in a "policy academy" to work on the project.

One of the states' tasks will be to improve collaboration among various agencies that all might have an interest in helping the same child. A lack of cooperation between social workers and educators is often blamed for gaps in children's learning.

And while the primary aim is to bring down the numbers of children in foster care, the initiative also will seek to improve school performance, said Joan Smith, the senior director of systems improvement at Casey Family Programs, a partner in the project.

In addition, at least two of the states, Pennsylvania and Ohio, have included education officials as team members.

## Scarce Resources

In California, which is home to more than 10 percent of the nation's children in foster care, the recent report by education and mental-health experts outlines a variety of strategies that policy makers and practitioners can use to reverse the many learning deficits among such children.

The report is the culmination of work conducted in 2005 and 2007 by the California Education Collaborative for Children in Foster Care, a committee that included child-welfare and education experts, former foster children, lawyers, and researchers. The Stuart Foundation, based in San Francisco, has supported the project with a $326,000 grant.

It notes that children in foster care are more likely to repeat grades, to be in special education, and to leave school without a high school diploma.

---

*Social workers, foster parents, and other caregivers . . . should receive training on early brain development and the developmental problems that can occur for foster children.*

---

The authors place a special emphasis on making sure children under age 5—who make up 32 percent of the more than 74,000 foster children in the state—receive preschool and early-intervention services.

Social workers, foster parents, and other caregivers, the authors recommend, should receive training on early brain development and the developmental problems that can occur for foster children. Preschool slots should also be increased in neighborhoods with high concentrations of foster families, such as low-income and minority neighborhoods, the report says.

"This is a population," said Jane Henderson, a consultant who worked on the California report, "that already qualifies for a lot of special services."

California and Delaware also have taken steps to allow children to stay in the schools they were attending before being placed in foster care, an effort to address the problem of high mobility that can disrupt children's education.

"That is a discussion that is happening in a lot of jurisdictions," added Robin Nixon, the executive director of the Washington-based National Foster Care Coalition, an advocacy organization.

But Ms. Henderson said that a 2003 California law never specified who would cover the cost of transportation if children are placed in foster homes outside their schools' attendance zones.

Ms. Henderson noted that while California's multibillion-dollar budget deficit won't allow for major new initiatives in this area, existing legislation could be more fully implemented.

California's 2003 law also allows for foster children to enroll in schools even if they lack the proper records and for students to receive partial credit for a course. But advocates say there is sometimes still resistance among school staff regarding such matters, and that more awareness is needed.

"There is so little sunshine on the issue, and the kids are kind of invisible, and they get bounced around," Ms. Henderson said.

## Educational Services Need a Higher Profile

Ms. Nixon and other advocates say they have seen an increase in efforts elsewhere to elevate foster children's educational needs.

Eight years ago, Advocates for Children of New York—a nonprofit organization that focuses on securing educational services for children at risk of school failure—was trying to get New York City child-welfare agencies to share data on children in foster care.

The intention was to better understand the educational needs of those students, many of whom qualify for special education services.

The advocacy group ran a pilot project from 2002 to 2004 in the now-closed Louise Wise Services, a child-welfare agency, in which members of the group's staff, including education lawyers, were placed inside the agency to focus on children's academic needs.

Advocates for Children made a big push to make sure the child welfare agencies in the city were enrolling children in tutoring services under the No Child Left Behind Act, said Gisela Alvarez, a senior project officer at the organization.

The city has even created an education unit within its Administration for Children's Services, which contracts with agencies to handle child placements.

"Just the presence of having someone focused on education really changed the culture of the agency," said Ms. Alvarez.

13

# Schools Do Not Meet the Special Education Needs of Foster Children

***Sarah Geenan and Laurie E. Powers***

*Sarah Geenan is an assistant professor and Laurie E. Powers is a professor at the Portland State University-Regional Research Institute.*

*While foster youths generally face greater academic challenges than their peers do, foster youths with disabilities and special education needs are particularly disadvantaged. Children who experience multiple foster placements often have to adjust to new schools as well, and some are entirely without direct adult support—a necessary element for the success of students with individualized education plans. Each academic milestone in a foster youth's life is crucial because education may be one of the only resources they can count on for their future success. Educators must give greater attention to special education needs, and caseworkers and foster parents must have adequate training so that they can be active allies for foster youth improvement.*

The scant information that is available suggests that the needs of foster care youths with disabilities are too often ignored or ineffectively addressed within the educational system. For example, a survey conducted in Oregon found that although 39 percent of youths in foster care had an individu-

Sarah Geenan and Laurie E. Powers, "Are We Ignoring Youths with Disabilities in Foster Care? An Examination of Their School Performance," *Social Work Research*, vol. 51, July 2006, pp. 233–41. 

alized education plan (IEP), only 16 percent actually received services. The special education system emphasizes, and is compelled to a large extent, by parental advocacy and participation. Although the Individuals with Disabilities Education Act requires that an educational surrogate must be appointed in a timely fashion when a biological parent is unavailable, evidence indicates that for foster youths in special education, a consistent, involved advocate typically does not exist. For example, although, foster parents often serve as educational surrogates, a study by the Advocates for Children of New York found that 90 percent, of foster parents reported that they had no involvement in the special education process. The educational experiences of foster youths in special education are also affected by their high mobility. A change in foster placement frequently means a change in schools and when paperwork does not follow the student promptly (as is often the case), staff members of the new school have little or no information about the special education needs of the transferring foster student. This lag often results in students being placed in inappropriate settings or programs and their IEPs not being implemented.

---

*Although education may be the most important bridge that foster youths have to successful adult life, many foster youths who also experience disability are stumbling before they get across.*

---

The education of the foster care youths with disabilities may frequently be overlooked in child welfare as well. One study revealed, for example, that caseworkers underestimated the number of foster children who receive special education by six-fold. The lack of awareness that caseworkers have regarding the special education needs of foster youths may reflect a pervasive lack of focus on the education of foster youths in general, regardless of disability. . . .

The educational performance of foster care youths in general has been substantially investigated, and research indicates that this group of students is struggling in school. . . .

In contrast, little is known about the educational performance of foster care youths in special education, and the few studies that have investigated this area have been limited by small samples. . . .

## Educational Accomplishment Is Essential for Foster Children

Although school success is a critical factor for all students in achieving positive adult outcomes, educational accomplishment may be particularly important for youths in foster care, who when transitioning to adulthood may have little else to draw upon. Every year, approximately 20,000 youths are emancipated from the child welfare system when they reach the age of majority (typically age 18), and frequently they enter adult life with little to no financial resources, community connection, or help from family. The odds for successful transition into adulthood are often stacked against foster youths, and research investigating the outcomes of these youths is troubling. A national study of former foster youths, ages 18 to 24, who had aged out of the child welfare system found that 2 1/2 to four years after leaving care, 30 percent were receiving public assistance, 50 percent had used illegal drugs, and 25 percent had been homeless at least one night. Furthermore, foster youths with disabilities (emotional, chronic health, physical, or developmental disabilities) demonstrated significantly poorer outcomes than their peers in foster care who did not have identified disabilities. Perhaps most important, research investigating resilience among foster care youths has demonstrated that educational achievement (for example, high school completion) is one of the best predictors of positive adult outcomes such as employment and postsecondary education.

Although education may be the most important bridge that foster youths have to successful adult life, many foster youths who also experience disability are stumbling before they get across, as the whipsaw effect of both foster care and special education may place them at even further risk of academic failure. The purpose of this study was to investigate the educational performance of foster youths in special education. Specifically, the study examined the extent to which the educational achievement of foster youths in special education differs from the academic performance of youths in foster care alone, youths in special education alone, and youths in general education (not foster care or special education). . . .

## Study Participants

Among the 327 students participating in the study, 59.6 percent were boys. The study's groups varied somewhat by gender: the special education groups (special education only and foster care and special education) had a larger percentage of males. This reflects national statistics, which indicate that boys receive special education services at twice the rate of girls. In terms of race and ethnicity, 176 participants were white, 109 were African American, 16 were Hispanic, 16 were Asian, and 10 were Native American. The foster care groups (foster care only and foster care and special education) had a larger percentage of African American students; this difference is consistent with the over-representation of African American youths in foster care on a national level. The average age of participants was 14.9, and the average grade level was 9.67. Although detailed information on the socio-economic status of participants was not available, the school district indicated which students received free or reduced lunch at school. This included all youths in the foster care groups (foster care only and foster care and special education), 22 youths in special education only, and eight youths in general education only. Among foster care youths, the median length of time in care was 133 weeks, with most youths (72 percent) experiencing one to four placements. The majority of these youths (79 percent) were in a nonrelative foster care placement.

---

*With regard to foster care experience, the findings indicated that as the number of youth foster placements increases, GPA and performance on state testing in math decreases.*

---

## Foster Care Children with Disabilities Fall Behind

The purpose of this study was to investigate the academic achievement of youths involved in foster care *and* special education, both in absolute terms and in comparison with their peers who experienced *only* foster care, special education, or general education. Consistent with other research, we found that a large percentage of youths in foster care were receiving special education services (44 percent). The results also indicated that foster care youths with disabilities performed poorly in school, lagged behind their peers in a number of important indices of academic achievement, and experienced significant challenges to educational success. For example, youths in foster care with disabilities had lower GPAs [grade point averages] than youths in general education, changed schools more frequently than youths in general education and special education only, earned fewer credits toward graduation than youths in general education, had lower scores on state testing, and were more likely to be exempted from testing than youths in general education and foster care only. In comparison with other students with disabilities, foster youths experienced more restrictive special education placements. In contrast to other youths in care, foster youths with disabilities had more foster home placements. With regard to foster care experience, the findings indicated that as the number of youth foster placements increases, GPA and performance on state testing in math decreases. The results also suggested that youths placed in nonrelative care (compared with kinship) had higher GPAs and a greater number of credits towards graduation. . . .

*Instability in foster care, which is typically associated with a change in schools, creates educational challenges for all foster youths.*

The findings suggest serious cause for concern regarding the academic performance of foster care youths in general, and foster youths with disabilities in particular. Although foster care or special education status alone appears to place a student at greater risk for academic difficulties, the negative impact of interfacing with both systems is multiplicative. These youths appear to be experiencing a whipsaw effect as they simultaneously face challenges related to special education and foster care separately, as well as the interaction between the two. An example of this multiplicative effect can be found in the higher rate of foster placement turnover among foster youths with disabilities. Instability in foster care, which is typically associated with a change in schools, creates educational challenges for all foster youths, but adjusting to a new educational setting may be especially difficult for a foster youth with a disability. The new school may be unaware of his or her special education needs and fail to provide necessary educational supports as stipulated in the student's IEP. Such problems in providing appropriate special education support may become compounded over time as foster youths with disabilities are more likely to experience multiple care placements. In turn, they may be more likely to experience instability in care because their foster parents lack the training, support, and resources necessary to address their special needs. . . .

Greater attention, commitment, and time must be given to the educational needs of foster care youths with disabilities in general education, special education, and child welfare. At a very basic level, there is a need for timely exchange of information between systems. . . . Educators need to know which students are in foster care, and child welfare professionals need to have information about a youth's disability needs and involvement in special education. Legislative barriers that make this exchange of information difficult must be addressed. Limited opportunities for schools and child protection agencies to collaborate are emerging, but educators and child welfare professionals must be proactive and work to engage one another if partnerships are to form. For example, as mentioned earlier, the transition planning and services that are offered through foster care independent living programs are rarely connected to the transition planning and services that occur through special education. Furthermore, there is a strong need to train educators on how to support the specific education and transition needs of foster youths. . . . Similarly, professionals in child welfare require education and training on the disability-related needs of youths. This information is critical for caseworkers' effective planning and support for youths in care, such as in selecting the best foster care placement and in appropriately interpreting and responding to problems that arise. Training should also be offered to foster parents and educational surrogates regarding how to advocate effectively for foster youths in the special education process. Foster parents and surrogates must be informed that youths are eligible for special education services and of how the system works if they are to have any chance to be an ally for the youths.

# 14

# Privatized Foster Care Is Increasing

***Laurent Belsie***

*Laurent Belsie is a staff writer for* The Christian Science Monitor.

*In an attempt to privatize child welfare, Kansas implemented a plan which would provide private companies a large sum for each child housed with a private agency. The new system aims to give agencies incentives to place children in homes more quickly. Laurent Belsie, author of this article, reports that while the changes in Kansas' child welfare system has shown some improvements, there are still many challenges. These challenges and the monetary loss associated with certain private agencies have surpassed any progress and success.*

It was billed as the grand experiment in privatizing child welfare.

Kansas would bid out adoption, foster care, and other services to private companies. They'd be paid a lump sum for each child. It was up to them to figure out how to deal with the caseload.

But somewhere between idea and implementation, things went wrong.

Without question, there have been significant advances. Among other things, Kansas has leveled the imbalance in ser-

Laurent Belsie, "Kansas' Bold Experiment in Child Welfare," *The Christian Science Monitor*, August 3, 2000. Reproduced by permission from Christian Science Monitor, (www.csmonitor.com).

vices between poorly served rural areas and better-served cities, and adoptions are up 81 percent.

## Changes in Child Welfare Do Not Live Up to Expectations

Yet the much-anticipated revolution in child welfare never occurred. Instead of creating a managed care system similar to a health-maintenance organization, the changes yielded only a semi-privatized system. Moreover, with one of the original private contractors now teetering on the edge of bankruptcy, the state has taken a step back from some of its boldest reforms.

As the presidential candidates begin to debate in earnest privatizing more social services, Kansas is a cautionary tale about the limits of privatization. It raises questions about whether some social responsibilities such as the welfare of children—sit uneasily on private shoulders.

"Kansas was everybody's poster boy for managed care," says Alfred Kahn, professor emeritus at Columbia University in New York and co-author of a forthcoming report on privatization. "And they have nothing to show for it yet that anybody should copy."

*The goal was to provide a monetary incentive for the agency to find homes for children as soon as possible.*

## Goals and Progress of Child Welfare Changes

Kansas' managed-care plan was set up on the innovative idea that each child in the adoption system came with roughly $13,500 in funding. The state would pay the private agency caring for the child half that amount when the child entered the system, another 25 percent when they were placed with adoptive parents, and the final 25 percent when the adoption became legal.

The goal was to provide a monetary incentive for the agency to find homes for children as soon as possible.

And the new system has made progress.

In addition to the leveling of urban and rural services and the improved adoption rate, the program is moving children back to their original families or adoptive parents more quickly. The state is also offering more services to more children than ever, and it is collecting far better data so it can hold contractors accountable to its new goals for child placement.

"The system was so significantly underfunded in Kansas," says Joyce Allegrucci, assistant secretary for children and family policy at the state's Department of Social and Rehabilitation Services in Topeka. "We have significantly more resources for children in this state than ever before."

## Challenges of the Changes

But recently, burgeoning problems have overshadowed the successes. Unable to move some hard-to-adopt children into new homes, the agency that has run Kansas' adoption program, Lutheran Social Services, has piled up huge debts.

Another challenge: the new process in 1996 was so different from the old system that no one knew how much it would cost, so monetary figures were just officials' best estimates.

As the costs became clearer, the state gave out more money—foster care funding alone has jumped nearly 17 percent since the new program took effect four years ago. But the increases haven't been enough to slow Lutheran Social Services' losses.

Late last month [July 2000], Lutheran Social Services of Kansas and Oklahoma told its subcontractors it had only $7.3 million to pay off some $9.8 million in debt. It has offered to pay its subcontractors 74 cents on the dollar.

Such a deal would be a big blow to some subcontractors, many of them local agencies providing various services for children. But if they don't accept, Lutheran Social Services could file for bankruptcy.

The company's biggest problem: cash flow, says Marc Bloomingdale, chief operating officer for the Wichita, Kan., agency.

Such funding problems have led the state to back away from its managed-care approach. In its latest round of contracts, which took effect in July [2000], agencies get a specific amount of money per month per child, not the lump $13,500 sum. It's a more traditional approach.

The change removes some of the incentive to move children quickly through the system. But officials hope federal regulations, which force states to integrate children quickly back into families or risk losing federal funds, will ensure that agencies don't simply stall so that they can receive more monthly payments.

---

*Under the old system, the facility might serve 70 different teenage girls in a year.*

---

Some experts in Kansas say slowing down a bit might be beneficial. While the fast-track approach works for most children, Kansas was in too much of a hurry at times, they say.

"I don't care how much training I have, there are certain kids I can't handle!" says Deborah Edelman-Dolan, a foster parent and clinical social worker at Florence Crittenton Services here in Topeka.

Recently, a caseworker contracted by the state urged her and her husband to take in a 14-year-old sexual offender. It was an inappropriate request for a family with two children of their own. Ms. Edelman-Dolan turned the caseworker down.

Private caseworkers and the state's representatives also depend on cursory evaluations at times.

For example, last week after a 30-minute and a 90-minute conversation with a troubled teen at Florence Crittenton, both the agency and the state caseworkers recommended she move to foster care. Critics say the examination was too hasty.

"We know what kids need," says Karen Shectman, executive director of Florence Crittenton.

Under the old system, the facility might serve 70 different teenage girls in a year. Now, it treats some 90 girls and for shorter periods of time. A half dozen have returned after foster homes didn't work out—something that rarely happened under the old system.

## Privatization Needs Time

The new system has also added another layer of bureaucracy—big contractors—between the state and local care givers. That has caused delays.

More often in recent years, district court Judge Dan Mitchell has found that his orders to get children evaluated or to put adults in parenting classes get delayed because the programs have long waiting lists.

"If we're going to make the effort to intervene, then we ought to be able to deliver and do it in a timely manner," says Judge Mitchell, who is assigned to the juvenile division in Shawnee County, which includes Topeka. "And that's not the case."

Supporters of the program, meanwhile, argue the system takes time to work out the kinks.

Privatization "makes sense," says Bob Smith, who heads United Methodist Youthville, a nonprofit child-welfare group that handles foster care for Wichita and surrounding Sedgwick County. "I don't feel it saves money initially. [But] you have the opportunity to create a model of service delivery that will be more efficient."

# Organizations to Contact

*The editors have compiled the following list of organizations concerned with the issues debated in this book. The descriptions are derived from materials provided by the organizations. All have publications or information available for interested readers. The list was compiled on the date of publication of the present volume; the information provided here may change. Be aware that many organizations take several weeks or longer to respond to inquiries, so allow as much time as possible.*

**Adoption History Project**
Department of History, University of Oregon
Eugene, OR 97403-1288
(541) 346-3118
e-mail: adoption@uoregon.edu
Web site: http://darkwing.uoregon.edu

The Adoption History Project introduces the history of child adoption in the United States by profiling people, organizations, topics, and studies that shaped adoption during the twentieth century. It is also intended for students and teachers interested in social welfare, the human sciences, and the history of children and families in the modern United States. The project offers a range of primary sources—published and unpublished documents, and images of people and organizations prominent in the child welfare system.

**American Bar Association (ABA) Center on Children and the Law**
740 Fifteenth Street NW, Washington, DC 20005
(800) 285-2221
e-mail: ctrchildlaw@abanet.org

The American Bar Association (ABA) Center on Children and the Law provides assistance, training, and research on court-related topics affecting children. These topics include child abuse and neglect, adoption, adolescent and infant/toddler health, foster and kinship care, juvenile status offenders, custody and support, guardianship, missing and exploited children, and children's exposure to domestic violence. The center's primary educational resource is its monthly *ABA Child Law Practice* publication. It also produces a free periodical on court system improvement, the *ABA Child CourtWorks,* and co-edits the *Children's Legal Rights Journal.*

**Casey Family Programs**

1300 Dexter Avenue N, 3rd Floor, Seattle, WA 98109-3542
(206) 282-7300
e-mail: info@casey.org
Web site: www.casey.org

Casey Family Programs provides an array of services for children and youth, with foster care as its core. Casey services include adoption, guardianship, kinship care, and family reunification. Casey is also committed to helping youth in foster care make a successful transition to adulthood. Some of the publications available online include *Casey Family Programs Tools and Resource Brochure, Better Together Resource Guide*, and *Court-Based Education Efforts for Children in Foster Care.*

**Center for the Study of Biracial Children**

2300 South Krameria Street, Denver, CO 80222
Web site: http://csbchome.org

The Center for the Study of Biracial Children produces and disseminates materials for and about interracial families and biracial children. The center provides advocacy, training, and consulting. Its primary mission is to advocate for the rights of interracial families, biracial children, and multiracial people. The Web site provides access to full-text articles, including: "Raising Successful Multiracial Children" and "Does Race Matter? Responding to Racial and Ethnic Diversity in Schools and Early Childhood Programs."

**Child Welfare Information Gateway**
1250 Maryland Avenue SW, 8th Floor
Washington, DC 20024
(703) 385-7565 or (800) 394-3366
e-mail: info@childwelfare.gov
Web site: www.childwelfare.gov

The Child Welfare Information Gateway provides access to print and electronic publications, Web sites, and online databases covering a wide range of topics, including child welfare, child abuse and neglect, and adoption. The Web site provides access to research, statistics, laws, and policies. The publications *Children's Bureau Express* and the *Sharing Family Strengths Activity Booklet* are available on the organization's Web site.

**Child Welfare League of America (CWLA)**
2345 Crystal Drive, Suite 250, Arlington, VA 22202
(703) 412-2400 • fax: (703) 412-2401
Web site: www.cwla.org

The Child Welfare League of America (CWLA) is the nation's oldest and largest membership-based child welfare organization. Since 1920, this coalition of hundreds of private and public agencies has worked to ensure safety, permanence, and well-being of children, youth, and their families. *The Kinship Reporter*, *A Community Outreach Handbook for Recruiting Foster Parents and Volunteers*, and *Children's Voice* magazine are examples of publications on the organization's Web site.

**Connect for Kids**
1625 K Street NW, 11th Floor, Washington, DC 20006
Web site: www.connectforkids.org

Connect for Kids serves a wide audience, ranging from professional child advocates to parents. Its Web site features original and reprinted articles and state-by-state listings of foster care organizations. The biweekly newsletter *CFK Update*, which presents and organizes the latest news, research, emerging trends, and policy developments affecting children, youth, families and communities is available on its Web site.

**National Association of Social Workers (NASW)**
750 First Street NE, Suite 700, Washington, DC 20002-4241
(202) 408-8600
Web site: www.socialworkers.org/

The National Association of Social Workers (NASW) works to enhance the professional growth and development of its members, to create and maintain professional standards, and to advance sound social policies. The Web site provides full-text access to the organization's newsletter, *NASW News.*

**National Court Appointed Special Advocates for Children (CASA)**
100 West Harrison North Tower, Suite 500
Seattle, WA 98119
(800) 628-3233
e-mail: staff@nationalcasa.org
Web site: www.nationalcasa.org

National Court Appointed Special Advocates for Children (CASA) is a network of more than 50,000 volunteers that serve 225,000 abused and neglected children through 900+ local program offices nationwide. Also known as guardians ad litem, CASA volunteers are appointed by judges to advocate for abused and neglected children. They stay with each case until it is closed, and the child is placed in a safe, permanent home. Online full-text publications include *Powerful Voice* and *The Connection.*

**National Foster Parent Association (NFPA)**
2313 Tacoma Avenue S, Tacoma, WA 98402
(800) 557-5238 • fax: (253) 683-4249
e-mail: info@nfpaonline.org
Web site: www.nfpainc.org

The mission of the National Foster Parent Association (NFPA) is to support foster parents in achieving safety, permanence, and well-being for the children and youth in their care. NFPA develops and provides education and training information and makes this information available to the public. Its quarterly publication, *National Advocate*, is a resource for foster and adoptive parents, child and family advocates, and child welfare agencies.

**National Network for Young People in Foster Care**
753 First Avenue, Seaside, OR 97138
(503) 717-1552 • fax: (503) 717-1702
Web site: www.fosterclub.com

National Network for Young People in Foster Care's Web sites, publications, and events provide a youth-friendly network that helps young people in foster care. The FosterClub is a peer support network that provides the tools, training, and forum to help young people secure a brighter future for themselves and the foster care system. The Web site provides a state-by-state guide to resources and access to the FosterClub program.

**U.S. Department of Health and Human Services**
**Administration for Children and Families**
370 L'Enfant Promenade SW, Washington, DC 20201
Web site: www.acf.hhs.gov

The Administration for Children and Families (ACF), within the U.S. Department of Health and Human Services (HHS), is responsible for federal programs that promote the economic and social well-being of families, children, individuals, and communities. Factsheets, Head Start publications, and research reports are available on its Web site.

# Bibliography

## Books


| | |
|---|---|
| Nina Bernstein | *The Lost Children of Wilder: The Epic Struggle to Change Foster Care*. New York: Pantheon Books, 2001. |
| Martha Randolph Carr | *A Place to Call Home: The Amazing Success Story of Modern Orphanages*. Amherst, NY: Prometheus Books, 2007. |
| Amy Coughlin and Caryn Abramowitz | *Cross-Cultural Adoption: How to Answer Questions from Family, Friends, and Community*. Washington, DC: LifeLine Press, 2004. |
| John Edwards, Marion Crain, and Arne L. Kalleberg, eds. | *Ending Poverty in America: How to Restore the American Dream*. New York: New Press, 2007. |
| Joyce E. Everett, Sandra S. Chipungu, and Bogart Leashore, eds. | *Child Welfare Revisited: An Africenteric Perspective*. New Brunswick, NJ: Rutgers University Press, 2004. |
| Madelyn Freundlich and Sarah Gerstenzang | *An Assessment of the Privatization of Child Welfare Services: Challenges and Successes*. Washington, DC: Child Welfare League of America, 2003. |

| | |
|---|---|
| Tim Giago | *Children Left Behind: The Dark Legacy of Indian Mission Boarding Schools*. Santa Fe, NM: Clear Light Publishing, 2006. |
| Ellen Herman | *Kinship by Design: A History of Adoption in the Modern United States.* Chicago, IL: University of Chicago Press, 2008. |
| Marilyn Irvin Holt | *Indian Orphanages*. Lawrence, KS: University Press of Kansas, 2004. |
| Margaret C. Jasper | *Custodial Rights*. Dobbs Ferry, NY: Oceana Publications, 2006. |
| B.J. Jones | *The Indian Child Welfare Act Handbook, Second Edition: A Legal Guide to the Custody and Adoption of Native American Children*. Chicago, IL: American Bar Association, 2008. |
| Betsy Krebs and Paul Pitcoff | *Beyond the Foster Care System: The Future for Teens*. New Brunswick, NJ: Rutgers University Press, 2006. |
| Janice Levy | *Finding the Right Spot: When Kids Can't Live with Their Parents.* Washington, DC: Magination Press, 2004. |
| Joyce Libal | *A House Between Homes: Youth in the Foster Care System*. Broomall, PA: Mason Crest Publishers, 2004. |
| Kathleen M. McNaught | *Learning Curves: Education Advocacy for Children in Foster Care.* Washington, DC: ABA Center On Children and the Law, 2004. |

| | |
|---|---|
| John T. Pardeck | *Children's Rights: Policy and Practice.* New York: Social Work Practice Press, 2006. |
| Lee Rainwater | *Poor Kids in a Rich Country: America's Children in Comparative Perspective.* New York: Russell Sage, 2003. |
| Catherine Reef | *Alone in the World: Orphans and Orphanages in America.* New York: Clarion Books, 2005. |
| Jennifer A. Reich | *Fixing Families: Parents, Power and the Child Welfare System.* New York: Routledge, 2005. |
| Dorothy E. Roberts | *Shattered Bonds: The Color of Child Welfare.* New York: Basic Books, 2002. |
| Barbara Katz Rothman | *Weaving a Family: Untangling Race and Adoption.* Boston, MA: Beacon Press Books, 2005. |
| Martha Shirk and Gary Stangler | *On Their Own: What Happens to Kids When They Age Out of the Foster Care System.* Boulder, CO: Westview Press, 2004. |


## Periodicals


| | |
|---|---|
| *American School Board Journal* | "Dropouts Decline, but Children in Poverty Increasing," September 2007. |

Gloria Batiste-Roberts — "Should Black Children Only Be Adopted by Black Parents? Yes, They Must Be Taught Coping Techniques to Deal with Racist Practices," *Ebony*, September 2008.

Nate Berg — "Who's Poor? It Depends on Where You Live, Some Say," *The Christian Science Monitor*, August 26, 2008.

Julie Bosman — "Study Reveals Harsh Life for Homeless Youth in New York," *The New York Times*, March 10, 2009.

Steve Christian — "Foster Care vs. Families," *State Legislatures*, June 2006.

Erik Eckholm — "Waits Plague Transfers of Children to Relatives' Care," *The New York Times*, June 27, 2008.

Gregory K. Fritz — "How the Foster Care System Fails Our Children," *Brown University Child and Adolescent Behavior Letter*, August 2008.

*Indian Country Today* — "Startling Demographics," September 10, 2008.

Demetria Irwin — "Parents Rally to Get Children Back from ACS," *New Amsterdam News*, September 25, 2008.

Karen Jowers — "Former Foster Children Find Sense of Family," *Air Force Times*, December 10, 2007.

Gordon E. Limb, David R. Hodge, and Patrick Panos "Social Work with Native People: Orienting Child Welfare Workers to the Beliefs, Values, and Practices of Native American People," *Journal of Public Child Welfare*, 2008.

Andrew O. Moore "Cities Support Transitions for Older Foster Youth," *Nation's Cities Weekly*, May 12, 2008.

Roberta Munroe "Race Relations," *Advocate*, August 28, 2007.

Marti Parham "Foster Care Adoption Gives Families an Option," *Jet*, December 8, 2008.

*Policy & Practice of Public Human Services* "Time for Reform: Investing in Prevention, Keeping Children Safe at Home," March 2008.

Nicole Marie Richardson "Adopt A Child: Black Children Flood the Foster Care System," *Black Enterprise*, May 2008.

Anna Rockhill, Beth L. Green, and Linda Newton-Curtis "Accessing Substance Abuse Treatment: Issues for Parents Involved with Child Welfare Services," *Child Welfare*, May/June 2008.

Gina Shaw "This Is What Adoption Feels Like," *Redbook*, November 2007.

*USA Today Magazine* "Foster Care Survivor Decries Conditions," July 2008.

Debra Viadero "Poor Rural Children Attract Close Study," *Education Week*, February 6, 2008.

| | |
|---|---|
| Mary Wakefield | "After Baby P: The Crisis in Child Foster Care," *Spectator*, December 6, 2008. |
| H. Barry Waldman, Stephen Perlman, and Cindy S. Lederman | "Foster Children with Disabilities," *Exceptional Parent*, December 2007. |
| Melissa Walker | "I'm Raising My Brother and Sister," *Cosmo Girl*, February 2008. |
| Kevin D. Williamson | "Lost Generation," *National Review*, August 4, 2008. |
| Wendy L. Wilson | "Kicked Out," *Essence*, September 2008. |

# Index

## D



## E



## F

## G



## H



## I



## J



## K



## L